CAMBRIDGE LIBRARY COLLECTION

Books of enduring scholarly value

History

The books reissued in this series include accounts of historical events and movements by eye-witnesses and contemporaries, as well as landmark studies that assembled significant source materials or developed new historiographical methods. The series includes work in social, political and military history on a wide range of periods and regions, giving modern scholars ready access to influential publications of the past.

Washington's Political Legacies

This collection of some of the most important letters and speeches of George Washington (1732–99) documents key moments of his military and political career as a general in the American army during the War of Independence and as the first President of the United States. Published in 1800 following Washington's death, this collection is dedicated to his widow Martha, and contains details of Washington's state funeral and memorial, and letters of condolence. The book includes a short biography covering the triumphs and tribulations of the war and presidency and describing the dedication to his country that caused Washington to be referred to as the 'Father of Our Country'. The public letters and speeches that Washington gave to Congress, the army and the public, such as *The Address on The Cessation of Hostilities*, mark a turning point in American history and the establishment of the modern democracy.

Cambridge University Press has long been a pioneer in the reissuing of out-of-print titles from its own backlist, producing digital reprints of books that are still sought after by scholars and students but could not be reprinted economically using traditional technology. The Cambridge Library Collection extends this activity to a wider range of books which are still of importance to researchers and professionals, either for the source material they contain, or as landmarks in the history of their academic discipline.

Drawing from the world-renowned collections in the Cambridge University Library, and guided by the advice of experts in each subject area, Cambridge University Press is using state-of-the-art scanning machines in its own Printing House to capture the content of each book selected for inclusion. The files are processed to give a consistently clear, crisp image, and the books finished to the high quality standard for which the Press is recognised around the world. The latest print-on-demand technology ensures that the books will remain available indefinitely, and that orders for single or multiple copies can quickly be supplied.

The Cambridge Library Collection will bring back to life books of enduring scholarly value (including out-of-copyright works originally issued by other publishers) across a wide range of disciplines in the humanities and social sciences and in science and technology.

Washington's Political Legacies

With a Biographical Outline
of his Life and Character

GEORGE WASHINGTON

CAMBRIDGE
UNIVERSITY PRESS

CAMBRIDGE UNIVERSITY PRESS

Cambridge, New York, Melbourne, Madrid, Cape Town, Singapore,
São Paolo, Delhi, Dubai, Tokyo, Mexico City

Published in the United States of America by Cambridge University Press, New York

www.cambridge.org
Information on this title: www.cambridge.org/9781108025935

© in this compilation Cambridge University Press 2010

This edition first published 1800
This digitally printed version 2010

ISBN 978-1-108-02593-5 Paperback

Washington's

POLITICAL LEGACIES.

TO WHICH IS ANNEXED AN

Appendix,

CONTAINING AN ACCOUNT OF HIS *ILLNESS*,

DEATH, AND THE *NATIONAL TRIBUTES*

OF *RESPECT* PAID TO HIS MEMORY,

WITH A

Biographical Outline

OF HIS

LIFE AND CHARACTER.

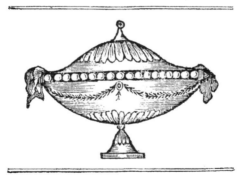

Boston,

PRINTED FOR *JOHN RUSSELL* AND *JOHN WEST*

1800.

MRS. WASHINGTON.

MADAM,

IN offering this Volume to your Patronage, and presenting it to the World under the Sanction of your NAME—a Name as endeared by Virtues, as illustrious from Glory—we feel that we are giving interest to excellence, and attaching tenderness to pre-eminence.

IN partaking the Solicitude, alleviating the Cares, and engaging the Confidence of that great, and disinterested Mind, which speaks in these pages, you have so well known to appreciate its Endowments, and to profit from the high Example, as to prefer the patriotic Duties to the selfifh Sensibilities, by resigning, to the claim of a Nation, that dear and solitary Sentiment, whose Hope, more strong than Death, would descend to the Tomb, mingle with the Ashes, and share the Sepulchre of departed affection.—Nor will you be divided—the Poet, and the Moralist, while they contemplate the *secluded Hero*, will perpetuate the *Charm* that gladdened, and the *Virtue* that rewarded every effort of a mind,which, commanding victory, and obtaining glory, could controul with temperance, and possess with moderation ; and which, at the dangerous summit of popular applause,was neither dazled by elevation, nor diminished by distance.

To you, the first mourner of a bereaved People, the melancholy consolation will remain, that a whole nation venerates your Virtues, and partakes your afflictions—Indeed every part of the civilized Earth will commemorate that excellence which cannot die—that MORTAL, who, born for the human race, crowned with its highest Homage, and graced with its best Exaltation, still instructs, and inspires, by the words of Wisdom, falling from the lips of IMMORTALITY.

WITH sympathy, sacred and devoted, with respect, veneration and gratitude, we remain, Madam, your obedient humble servants,

THE EDITORS.

BOSTON, MARCH, 1800.

ADVERTISEMENT.

THE compilers of this volume think proper to declare, that, in collecting the papers and materials which constitute its contents, they have used only those which the immortal WASHINGTON wrote, when it was in his great and wise mind to instruct, direct, and admonish his countrymen : they conceive that to have departed from this rule might have led them to matter, sufficiently abundant, to fill many volumes, and not so immediately connected with the public expectation. In this volume will be found all those great truths, and virtuous recommendations, which, if cherished and practised, must lead this nation to prosperity, happiness, and glory : the author of the biographical outline of General WASHINGTON, which forms a part of this work, is confessedly indebted, for his dates to the valuable publications of the rev. Dr. MORSE, MISS HANNAH ADAMS, and some European prints.

THE original proposal for publishing this work, promised The President's letter of condolence to Mrs. WASHINGTON ; but this could not be obtained—we are, however, authorised in saying, that his message to Congress, communicating that virtuous lady's answer, contains the spirit of it.

Boston, March 1800.

TABLE OF CONTENTS.

Washington's

POLITICAL LEGACIES.

IN CONGRESS,
Thursday, June 15, 1775.

Resolved, That a General be appointed to command all the continental forces, raised, or to be raised, for the defence of American liberty.

That five hundred dollars per month be allowed for the pay and expences of the general.

The Congress then proceeded to the choice of a General, by ballot, and *George Washington, Esq.* was unanimously elected.

Friday, June 16, 1775.

The President informed col. Washington that the Congress had, yesterday, unanimously made choice of him to be general and commander in chief of the American forces, and requested he would accept of that employment ; to which col. Washington, standing in his place, as a member of the house, answered :

B

" *MR. PRESIDENT,*

" THOUGH I am truly sensible of the high honour done me in this appointment, yet I feel great distress, from a consciousness that my abilities and military experience may not be equal to the extensive and important trust: however, as the Congress desire it, I will enter upon the momentous duty, and exert every power I possess, in their service, for support of the glorious cause. I beg they will accept my most cordial thanks for this distinguished testimony of their approbation.

" BUT, lest some event should happen unfavourable to my reputation, I beg it may be remembered by every gentleman in the room, that I, this day, declare with the utmost sincerity, I do not think myself equal to the command I am honoured with.

" WITH respect to pay, sir, I must beg leave to assure Congress, that as no pecuniary consideration could have tempted me to accept this arduous employment, at the expence of my domestic ease and happiness, I do not wish to make any profit from it. I will keep an exact account of my expences. Those I doubt not they will discharge, and that is all I desire."

ON THE CESSATION OF HOSTILITIES, *GENE-RAL WASHINGTON* ISSUED THE FOLLOWING
ORDERS :

Head-Quarters, Newburg, April 18, 1783.

THE commander in chief orders the
cessation of hostilities between the United
States of America and the king of Great-Britain, to be publickly proclaimed to-morrow at 12 o'clock, at the new building ; and
that the proclamation which will be communicated herewith, be read to-morrow evening, at the head of every regiment and corps
of the army ; after which, the chaplains,
with the several brigades, will render thanks
to Almighty God for all his mercies, particularly for his over-ruling the wrath of man
to his own glory, and causing the rage of
war to cease amongst the nations.

ALTHOUGH the proclamation before alluded to, extends only to the prohibition of
hostilities, and not to the annunciation of a
general peace, yet it must afford the most
rational and sincere satisfaction to every benevolent mind, as it puts a period to a long
and doubtful contest—stops the effusion of
human blood—opens the prospect to a more
splendid scene—and, like another morning

star, promises the approach of a brighter
day than has hitherto illuminated this western hemisphere ! on such a happy day—a
day which is the harbinger of peace—a day
which completes the eighth year of the war,
it would be ingratitude not to rejoice : it
would be insensibility not to participate in
the general felicity.

THE commander in chief, far from en-
deavouring to stifle the feelings of joy in
his own bosom, offers his most cordial congratulations on the occasion, to all the officers of every denomination—to all the
troops of the United States in general, and
in particular to those gallant and persevering men, who had resolved to defend the
rights of their invaded country so long as
the war should continue ; for these are the
men who ought to be considered as the
pride and boast of the American army, and
who, crowned with well-earned laurels, may
soon withdraw from the field of glory to the
more tranquil walks of civil life.

WHILE the General recollects the almost
infinite variety of scenes through which we
have passed with a mixture of pleasure, astonishment and gratitude—while he con-

templates the prospects before us with rapture—he cannot help wishing that all the
brave men, of whatever condition they may
be, who have shared in the toils and dangers
of effecting this glorious revolution, of rescu-
ing millions from the hand of oppression,
and of laying the foundation of a great empire, might be impressed with a proper idea
of the dignified part they have been called to
act (under the smiles of providence) on the
stage of human affairs ; for happy, thrice
happy, shall they be pronounced hereafter,
who have contributed any thing, who have
performed the meanest office in erecting this
stupendous *fabric of Freedom and Empire*, on
the broad basis of independency ; who have
assisted in protecting the rights of human
nature, and establishing an asylum for the
poor and oppressed of all nations and reli-
gions.

THE glorious task for which we first flew
to arms, being thus accomplished—the liberties of our country being fully acknowledged and firmly secured, by the smiles of Heav-
en, on the purity of our cause, and the honest exertions of a feeble people, determined
to be free, against a powerful nation disposed
to oppress them ; and the character of those

who have persevered through every extremity of hardship, suffering, and danger, being immortalized by the illustrious appellation of the *Patriot Army*, nothing now remains but for the actors of this mighty scene to preserve a perfect, unvarying consistency of character through the very last act; to close the drama with applause; and to retire from the military theatre with the same approbation of angels and men, which have crowned all their former virtuous actions.

FOR this purpose, no disorder or licentiousness must be tolerated; every considerate and well-disposed soldier must remember, it will be absolutely necessary to wait with patience, until peace shall be declared, or Congress shall be enabled to take proper measures for the security of the public stores, &c. As soon as these arrangements shall be made, the General is confident there will be no delay in discharging, with every mark of distinction and honour, all the men enlisted for the war, who will then have faithfully performed their engagements with the public. The General has already interested himself in their behalf; and he thinks he need not repeat the assurances of his disposition to be useful to them on the present, and every other proper occasion.   In the mean time he is determined that no military neglects or excesses shall go unpunished, while he retains the command of the army.

THE adjutant-general will have such working-parties detached to assist in making the preparation for a general rejoicing, as the chief engineer, with the army, shall call for ; and the quarter-master-general will also furnish such materials as he may want. The quarter-master-general will, without delay, procure such a number of discharges to be printed as will be sufficient for all the men enlisted for the war ; he will please to apply to head-quarters for the form.

AN extra ration of liquor to be issued to every man to-morrow, to drink PERPETU-AL PEACE, INDEPENDENCE, AND HAP-PINESS TO THE UNITED STATES OF AMERICA.

A CIRCULAR LETTER,

FROM HIS EXCELLENCY *GEORGE WASHINGTON*,
COMMANDER IN CHIEF OF THE ARMIES OF
THE UNITED STATES OF AMERICA, TO THE
GOVERNORS OF THE SEVERAL STATES.

Head-Quarters, Newburg, June 18, 1783.

SIR,

THE great object for which I had the
honor to hold an appointment in the service
of my country, being accomplished, I am now
preparing to refign it into the hands of congress, and return to that domestic retirement,
which, it is well known, I left with the greatest reluctance ; a retirement for which I have
never ceased to sigh through a long and painful absence, in which (remote from the noise
and trouble of the world) I meditate to pass
the remainder of life in a state of undisturbed repose ; but, before I carry this resolution
into effect, I think it a duty incumbent on
me to make this my last official communication, to congratulate you on the glorious e-
vents which Heaven has been pleased to produce in our favour, to offer my sentiments
respecting some important subjects, which
appear to me to be intimately connected with
the tranquillity of the United States, to take
my leave of your Excellency as a public cha-

racter, and to give my final blessing to that
country in whose service I have spent the
prime of my life ; for whose sake I have
consumed so many anxious days and watch-
ful nights ; and whose happiness, being ex-
tremely dear to me,will always constitute no
inconsiderable part of my own.

IMPRESSED with the liveliest sensibility on
this pleasing occasion, I will claim the indulgence of dilating the more copiously on the
subject of our mutual felicitation.   When we
consider the magnitude of the prize we contended for, the doubtful nature of the contest,
and the favourable manner in which it has
terminated ; we shall find the greatest possible reason for gratitude and rejoicing : this
is a theme that will afford infinite delight to
every benevolent and liberal mind, whether
the event in contemplation be considered as
a source of present enjoyment, or the parent
of future happiness ; and we shall have equal
occasion to felicitate ourselves on the lot
which providence has assigned us, whether
we view it in a natural, a political, or moral
point of view.

THE citizens of America, placed in the
most enviable condition, as the sole lords and

proprietors of a vast tract of continent, comprehending all the various soils and climates
of the world, and abounding with all the necessaries and conveniencies of life, are now, by
the late satisfactory pacification, acknowledged
to be possessed of absolute freedom and independency; they are, from this period to be considered as the actors on a most conspicuous
theatre, which seems to be peculiarly designed by providence for the display of human
greatness and felicity : here they are not only
surrounded with every thing that can contribute to the completion of private and domestic enjoyment, but heaven has crowned all
its other blessings, by giving a surer opportunity for political happiness than any other
nation has ever been favoured with. Nothing can illustrate these observations more
forcibly than the recollection of the happy
conjuncture of times and circumstances, under which our republic assumed its rank a-
mong the nations. The foundation of our
empire was not laid in a gloomy age of igno-
rance and superstition, but at an epoch
when the rights of mankind were better understood, and more clearly defined than at
any former period : researches of the human
mind after social happiness have been carried

to a great extent : the treasures of knowledge acquired by the labours of philosophers,
sages, and legislators, through a long succession of years, are laid open for us, and their
collected wisdom may be happily applied in
the establishment of our forms of government : the free cultivation of letters, the un-
bounded extension of commerce, the progressive refinement of manners, the growing liberality of sentiment, and, above all,
the pure and benign light of revelation, have
had a meliorating influence on mankind, and
increased the blessings of society. At this
auspicious period the United States came into
existence as a nation, and if their citizens
should not be completely free and happy,
the fault will be entirely their own.

SUCH is our situation, and such are our
prospects ; but notwithstanding the cup of
blessing is thus reached out to us—notwithstanding happiness is ours, if we have a disposition to seize the occasion, and make it
our own ; yet it appears to me, there is an
option still left to the United States of America, whether they will be respectable and prosperous, or contemptible and miserable as a
nation. This is the time of their political pro-

bation ; this is the moment, when the eyes of
the whole world are turned upon them ;
this is the time to establifh or ruin their national character forever ; this is the favourable moment to give such a tone to the federal government, as will enable it to answer
the ends of its institution ; or this may be
the ill-fated moment for relaxing the powers of the union, annihilating the cement of
the confederation, and exposing us to become
the sport of European politics, which may
play one state against another, to prevent
their growing importance, and to serve their
own interested purposes. For, according to
the system of policy the states shall adopt at
this moment, they will stand or fall ; and,
by their confirmation or lapse, it is yet to be
decided, whether the revolution must ultimately be considered as a blessing or a curse;
a blessing or a curse, not to the present age
alone, for with our fate will the destiny of
unborn millions be involved.

WITH this conviction of the importance
of the present crisis, silence in me would
be a crime. I will therefore speak to your
Excellency the language of freedom and sincerity, without disguise. I am aware, how-

ever, those who differ from me in political
sentiments, may perhaps remark, I am step-
ping out of the proper line of my duty ; and
they may possibly ascribe to arrogance or
ostentation, what I know is alone the result
of the purest intention ; but the rectitude of
my own heart, which disdains such unworthy
motives—the part I have hitherto acted in
life—the determination I have formed of not
taking any fhare in public bufiness hereafter
—the ardent desire I feel and shall continue
to manifest, of quietly enjoying in private
life, after all the toils of war, the benefits of
a wise and liberal government—will, I flatter myself, sooner or later, convince my
countrymen, that I could have no sinister
views in delivering, with so little reserve,
the opinions contained in this Address.

THERE are four things which I humbly
conceive are essential to the well-being, I may
even venture to say, to the existence of the
United States, as an independent power.

1ſt. AN indissoluble union of the states
under one federal head.

2dly. A sacred regard to public justice.

3dly. THE adoption of a proper peace establishment. And,

4*thly.* THE prevalence of that pacific and
friendly disposition among the people of the
United States, which will induce them to forget their local prejudices and policies, to make
those mutual concessions which are requisite
to the general prosperity, and, in some instances, to sacrifice their individual advantages to the interest of the community.

THESE are the pillars on which the glorious fabric of our independency and national
character must be supported. Liberty is the
basis, and whoever would dare to sap the
foundation, or overturn the structure, under whatever specious pretext he may attempt it, will merit the bitterest execra-
tion and the severest punishment which can
be inflicted by his injured country.

ON the three first articles I will make a
few observations, leaving the last to the good
sense and serious consideration of those immediately concerned.

UNDER the first head, although it may
not be neceffary or proper for me in this
place to enter into a particular disquisition
of the principles of the union, and to take
up the great question which has been fre-

quently agitated, whether it be expedient
and requisite for the states to delegate a large
proportion of power to Congress, or not ;
yet it will be a part of my duty, and that of
every true patriot, to assert, without reserve,
and to insist upon the following positions.
That unless the states will suffer Congress to
exercise those prerogatives they are undoubtedly invested with by the constitution, every
thing must very rapidly tend to anarchy and
confusion.—That it is indispensable to the
happiness of the individual states, that there
should be lodged, somewhere, a supreme
power, to regulate and govern the general
concerns of the confederated republic, without which the union cannot be of long du-
ration.—That there must be a faithful and
pointed compliance on the part of every state
with the late proposals and demands of Congress, or the most fatal consequences will en-
sue.—That whatever measures have a tendency to dissolve the union, or contribute to
violate or lessen the sovereign authority,
ought to be considered as hostile to the liberty and independency of America, and the
authors of them treated accordingly.—And
lastly, that unless we can be enabled by the
concurrence of the states, to participate of the

fruits of the revolution, and enjoy the essential benefits of civil society, under a form of
government so free and uncorrupted, so happily guarded against the danger of oppression, as has been devised and adopted by the
articles of confederation, it will be a subject
of regret, that so much blood and treasure
have been lavished for no purpose ; that so
many sufferings have been encountered without a compensation, and that so many sacri-
fices have been made in vain. Many other
considerations might here be adduced to
prove, that without an entire conformity to
the spirit of the union, we cannot exist as an
independent power. It will be sufficient for
my purpose to mention but one or two,
which seem to me of the greatest importance.
It is only in our united character, as an empire, that our independence is acknowledged,
that our power can be regarded, or our credit supported among foreign nations. The
treaties of the European powers with the
United States of America, will have no va-
lidity on the dissolution of the union. We
shall be left nearly in a state of nature ; or
we may find, by our own unhappy experience, that there is a natural and necessary
progression from the extreme of anarchy to

the extreme of tyranny ; and that arbitrary power is most easily established on the ruins of liberty abused to licentiousness.

As to the second article, which respects the performance of public justice, Congress have, in their late Address to the United States, almost exhausted the subject ; they have explained their ideas so fully, and have enforced the obligations the states are under to render complete justice to all the public creditors, with so much dignity and energy, that in my opinion, no real friend to the honour and independency of America can hesitate a single moment respecting the propriety of complying with the just and honourable measures proposed. If their arguments do not produce conviction, I know of nothing that will have greater influence, especially when we reflect that the system referred to, being the result of the collected wisdom of the continent, must be esteemed, if not perfect, certainly the least objectionable of any that could be devised ; and that, if it should not be carried into immediate execution, a national bankruptcy, with all its deplorable consequences, will take place, before any different plan can possibly be pro-

posed or adopted ; so pressing are the present circumstances, and such is the alternative now offered to the states.

THE ability of the country to discharge
the debts which have been incurred in its
defence, is not to be doubted. An inclination, I flatter myself, will not be wanting ;
the path of our duty is plain before us ;
honesty will be found, on every experiment,
to be the best and only true policy. Let us
then, as a nation, be just ; let us fulfil the
public contracts which Congress had undoubtedly a right to make for the purpose of carrying on the war, with the same
good faith we suppose ourselves bound to
perform our private engagements. In the
mean time let an attention to the cheerful
performance of their proper business, as individuals, and as members of society, be
earnestly inculcated on the citizens of America ; then will they strengthen the bands of
government, and be happy under its protection. Every one will reap the fruit of his
labours ; every one will enjoy his own acquisitions, without molestation and without
danger.

IN this state of absolute freedom and perfect security, who will grudge to yield a
very little of his property to support the
common interests of society, and ensure the
protection of government ? who does not
remember the frequent declarations at the
commencement of the war, that we should
be completely satisfied, if at the expense of
one half, we could defend the remainder of
our possessions ? where is the man to be
found, who wishes to remain indebted for
the defence of his own person and property
to the exertions, the bravery, and the blood
of others, without making one generous effort to pay the debt of honour and of gratitude ? in what part of the continent shall we
find any man, or body of men, who would
not blush to stand up, and propose measures
purposely calculated to rob the soldier of his
stipend, and the public creditor of his due ?
And were it possible that such a flagrant instance of injustice could ever happen, would
it not excite the general indignation, and tend
to bring down upon the authors of such
measures, the aggravated vengeance of heav-
en ? If, after all, a spirit of disunion, or a
temper of obstinacy and perverseness should
manifest itself in any of the states ; if such

an ungracious disposition should attempt to
frustrate all the happy effects that might be
expected to flow from the union ; if there
should be a refusal to comply with the requisitions for funds to discharge the annual
interest of the public debts, and if that refu-
sal should revive all those jealousies, and
produce all those evils which are now happily removed—Congress, who have in all
their transactions shewn a great degree of
magnanimity and justice, will stand justified
in the sight of God and man ! And that State
alone, which puts itself in opposition to the
aggregate wisdom of the continent, and follows such mistaken and pernicious councils,
will be responsible for all the consequences.

FOR my own part, conscious of having
acted, while a servant of the public, in the
manner I conceived best suited to promote
the real interests of my country ; having,
in consequence of my fixed belief, in some
measure, pledged myself to the army, that
their country would finally do them complete and ample justice, and not willing to
conceal any instance of my official conduct
from the eyes of the world, I have thought
proper to transmit to your excellency the in-

closed collection of papers, relative to the
half-pay and commutation granted by Congress to the officers of the army : from these
communications, my decided sentiment will
be clearly comprehended, together with the
conclusive reasons, which induced me at an
early period, to reccommend the adoption of
this measure in the most earnest and serious
manner. As the proceedings of Congress, the
army, and myself, are open to all, and contain, in my opinion, sufficient information
to remove the prejudice and errors which
may have been entertained by any, I think
it unnecessary to say any thing more, than
just to observe, that the resolutions of Congress, now alluded to, are as undoubtedly
and absolutely binding upon the United States
as the most solemn acts of confederation or
legislation.

As to the idea, which I am informed, has in
some instances prevailed, that the half-pay
and commutation are to be regarded mere-
ly in the odious light of a pension, it ought
to be exploded forever : that provision
fhould be viewed, as it really was, a reasona-
ble compensation offered by Congress, at a
time when they had nothing else to give to

officers of the army, for services then to be
performed : it was the only means to prevent a total derileftion of the service ; it
was a part of their hire. I may be allowed
to say, it was the price of their blood, and
of your independency ; it is therefore more
than a common debt, it is a debt of honour ;
it can never be considered as a pension or
gratuity, nor cancelled until it is fairly dis-
charged.

WITH regard to the distinftion between officers and soldiers, it is sufficient that the u-
niform experience of every nation of the
world, combined with our own, proves the
utility and propriety of the discrimination,
Rewards, in proportion to the aid the public draws from them, are unquestionably due
to all its servants. In some lines, the soldiers have perhaps generally had as ample
compensation for their services, by the large
bounties which have been paid them, as their
officers will receive in the proposed commutation ; in others, if besides the donation of
land, the payment of arrearages of cloathing
and wages (in which articles all the component parts of the army must be put upon
the same footing) we take into the estimate,

the bounties many of the soldiers have received, and the gratuity of one year's full
pay, which is promised to all, possibly their
situation (every circumstance being duly
considered) will not be deemed less eligible
than that of the officers. Should a farther
reward, however, be judged equitable, I will
venture to assert, no man will enjoy greater
satisfaction than myself, in an exemption
from taxes for a limited time (which has
been petitioned for in some instances) or a-
ny other adequate immunity or compensation granted to the brave defenders of their
country's cause : but neither the adoption
or rejection of this proposition will, in any
manner affect, much less militate against the
act of Congress, by which they have offered
five years full pay, in lieu of the half-pay for
life, which had been before promised to the
officers of the army.

BEFORE I conclude the subject on public
juſtice, I cannot omit to mention the obligations this country is under to that meritori-
ous class of veterans, the non-commissioned
officers and privates, who have been dis-
charged for inability, in consequence of the
resolution of Congress, of the 23d of April,

1782, on an annual pension for life. Their
peculiar sufferings, their singular merits and
claims to that provision need only to be
known, to interest the feelings of humanity
in their behalf. Nothing but a punctual
payment of their annual allowance can res-
cue them from the most complicated mise-
ry ; and nothing could be a more melancholy and distressing sight, than to behold
those who have shed their blood, or lost
their limbs in the service of their country,
without a shelter, without a friend, and
without the means of obtaining any of the
comforts or necessaries of life, compelled to
beg their daily bread from door to door.
Suffer me to recommend those of this description, belonging to your state, to the
warmest patronage of your excellency and
your legislature.

IT is necessary to say but a few words on
the third topic which was proposed, and
which regards particularly the defence of the
republic. As there can be little doubt but
Congress will recommend a proper peace establishment for the United States, in which
a due attention will be paid to the importance of placing the militia of the union up-

on a regular and respectable footing ; if this
should be the case, I should beg leave to urge
the great advantage of it in the strongest
terms.

THE militia of this country must be considered as the palladium of our security, and
the first effectual resort in case of hostility :
it is essential, therefore, that the same system
should pervade the whole ; that the formation and discipline of the militia of the continent should be absolutely uniform ; and
that the same species of arms, accoutrements,
and military apparatus, should be introduced
in every part of the United States. No one,
who has not learned it from experience, can
conceive the difficulty, expense, and confusion which result from a contrary system, or
the vague arrangements which have hitherto
prevailed.

IF, in treating of political points, a greater latitude than usual has been taken in the
course of this Address, the importance of the
crisis, and the magnitude of the objects in
discussion, must be my apology : it is, however, neither my wish nor expectation, that
the preceding observations should claim any

E

regard, except so far as they shall appear to
be dictated by a good intention ; consonant
to the immutable rules of justice ; calculated
to produce a liberal system of policy, and
founded on whatever experience may have
been acquired by a long and close attention
to public business. Here I might speak with
more confidence, from my actual observations ; and if it would not swell this letter
(already too prolix) beyond the bounds I
had prescribed myself, I could demonstrate
to every mind, open to conviction, that in
less time, and with much less expense than
has been incurred, the war might have been
brought to the same happy conclusion, if the
resources of the continent could have been
properly called forth ; that the distresses and
disappointments which have very often occurred, have, in too many instances, resulted more from a want of energy in the continental government, than a deficiency of
means in the particular states : that the in-
efficacy of the measures, arising from the
want of an adequate authority in the supreme power, from a partial compliance with
the requisitions of Congress in some of the
states, and from a failure of punctuality in
others, while they tended to damp the zeal

of those who were more willing to exert themselves, served also to accumulate the expenses of the war, and to frustrate the best concerted plans ; and that the discouragement occasioned by the complicated difficulties and embarrassments, in which our affairs were by this means involved, would have long ago produced the dissolution of any army, less patient, less virtuous, and less persevering than that which I have had the honour-to command. But while I mention those things, which are notorious facts, as the defects of our federal constitution, particularly in the prosecution of a war, I beg it may be understood, that as I have ever taken a pleasure in gratefully acknowledging the assistance and support I have derived from every class of citizens ; so shall I always be happy to do justice to the unparalleled exertions of the individual states, on many interesting occasions.

I HAVE thus freely disclosed what I wished to make known before I surrendered up my public trust to those who committed it to me : the task is now accomplished. I now bid adieu to your excellency, as the chief magistrate of your state ; at the same time

I bid a last farewel to the cares of office, and all the employments of public life.

IT remains, then, to be my final and only request, that your excellency will communicate these sentiments to your legislature, at their next meeting ; and that they may be considered as the legacy of one who has ardently wished, on all occasions, to be useful to his country, and who, even in the shade of retirement, will not fail to implore the divine benediction upon it.

I NOW make it my earnest prayer, that God would have you, and the state over which you preside, in his holy protection ; that he would incline the hearts of the citizens to cultivate a spirit of subordination and obedience to government ; to entertain a brotherly affection and love for one another, for their fellow citizens of the United States at large ; and particularly for their brethren who have served in the field ; and finally, that he would most graciously be pleased to dispose us all to do justice, to love mercy, and to demean ourselves with that charity, humility, and pacific temper of the mind, which were the characteristics of the divine author of our blessed religion ; without an humble imitation of whose example, in these things, we can never hope to be a happy nation.

I HAVE the honour to be, with much esteem and respect, sir, your excellency's most obedient, and most humble servant,

G. WASHINGTON.

IN CONGRESS,

Princeton, Aug. 26, 1783.

GENERAL *WASHINGTON* BEING INTRODUCED
BY TWO MEMBERS, THE PRESIDENT ADDRES-
SED HIM AS FOLLOWS :

SIR,

Congress feel particular pleasure in seeing your excellency, and in congratulating you on the success of a war in which you have acted so conspicuous a part.

It has been the singular happiness of the United States, that during a war so long, so dangerous, and so important, Providence has been graciously pleased to preserve the life of a General, who has merited and possessed the uninterrupted confidence and affection of his fellow-citizens. In other nations many have performed services for which they have deserved and received the thanks of the public ; but to you, sir, peculiar praise is due, your services have been essential in acquiring and establishing the freedom and independence of your country ; they deserve the grateful acknowledgments of a free and independent nation : those acknowledgments Congress have the satisfaction of expressing to your excellency.

HOSTILITIES have now ceased, but your country still needs your services ; she wishes to avail herself of your talents in forming the arrangements which will be necessary for her in the time of peace ; for this reason your attendance at Congress has been requested. A committee is appointed to confer with your excellency, and to receive your assistance in preparing and adjusting plans relative to these important objects.

TO WHICH HIS EXCELLENCY MADE THE FOLLOWING REPLY.

MR. PRESIDENT,

I AM too sensible of the honourable reception I have now experienced, not to be penetrated with the deepest feelings of gratitude.

NOTWITHSTANDING Congress appear to estimate the value of my life beyond any services I have been able to render the United States, yet I must be permitted to consider the wisdom and unanimity of our national councils, the firmness of our citizens, and the patience and bravery of our troops, which have produced so happy a termination of the war, as the most conspicuous effect of the divine interposition, and the surest presage of our future happiness.

HIGHLY gratified by the favourable sentiments which Congress are pleased to express of my past conduct, and amply rewarded by the confidence and affection of my fellow citizens, I cannot hesitate to contribute my best endeavours towards the establishment of the national security in whatever manner the sovereign power may think proper to direct, until the ratification of the definitive treaty of peace, or the final evacuation of our country by the British forces ; after either of which events, I shall ask permission to retire to the peaceful shade of private life.

PERHAPS, sir, no occasion may offer more suitable than the present to express my humble thanks to God, and my grateful acknowledgments to my country, for the great and universal support I have received in every vicissitude of fortune, and for the many distinguished honours which Congress have been pleased to confer upon me in the course of the war.

FAREWELL ADDRESS

OF GENERAL *WASHINGTON* TO THE ARMIES OF
THE UNITED STATES.

Rocky-Hill, near Princeton, Nov. 2, 1783

THE United States in Congress assembled, after giving the most honourable testimony to the merits of the federal armies, and
presenting them with the thanks of their
country, for their long, eminent and faithful
service, having thought proper, by their proclamation bearing date the 18th of October
last, to discharge such part of the troops as
were engaged for the war, and to permit the
officers on furlough to retire from service,
from and after to-morrow, which proclamation having been communicated in the public papers for the information and government of all concerned ; it only remains for
the commander in chief to address himself
once more, and that for the last time, to the
armies of the United States, (however wide-
ly dispersed individuals who compose them
may be) and to bid them an affectionate, a
long farewel.

BUT before the commander in chief takes
his final leave of those he holds most dear,

F

he wishes to indulge himself a few moments
in calling to mind a slight review of the
past :—he will then take the liberty of ex-
ploring, with his military friends, their future prospects ; of advising the general line
of conduct which in his opinion ought to be
pursued ; and he will conclude the Address,
by expressing the obligations he feels himself
under for the spirited and able assistance he
has experienced from them, in the performance of an arduous office.

A CONTEMPLATION of the complete attainment (at a period earlier than could have
been expected) of the object for which we
contended against so formidable a power,
cannot but inspire us with astonishment and
gratitude. The disadvantageous circumstances on our part, with which the war
was undertaken, can never be forgotten.
The singular interposition of providence in
our feeble condition, were such as could
scarcely escape the attention of the most un-
observing—while the unparalleled perseverance of the armies of the United States,
through almost every possible suffering and
discouragement, for the space of eight long
years, was little short of a standing miracle.

IT is not the meaning, nor within the compass of this Address, to detail the hardships peculiarly incident to our service, or to describe the distresses which in several instances have resulted from the extremes of hunger and nakedness, combined with the rigours of an inclement season ; nor is it necessary to dwell on the dark side of our past affairs. Every American officer and soldier must now console himself for any unpleasant circumstances which may have occurred, by a recollection of the uncommon scenes in which he has been called to act no inglorious part, and the astonishing events of which he has been a witness ; events which have seldom, if ever before, taken place on the stage of human action, nor can they probably ever happen again. For who has before seen a disciplined army formed at once from such raw materials ? who that was not a witness could imagine that the most violent local prejudices would cease so soon, and that men who came from the different parts of the continent, strongly disposed by the habits of education to despise and quarrel with each other, would instantly become one patriotic band of brothets ? or who that was not on the spot, can trace the steps by which such a wonderful revolution has been effected, and such a glorious period put to all our warlike toils ?

IT is universally acknowledged, that the enlarged prospects of happiness, opened by the confirmation of our independence and sovereignty, almost exceed the power of description : and shall not the brave men who have contributed so essentially to these inestimable acquisitions, retiring victorious from the field of war to the field of agriculture, participate in all the blessings which have been obtained ? In such a republic, who will exclude them from the rights of citizens, and the fruits of their labours ? in such a country, so happily circumstanced, the pursuits of commerce, and the cultivation of the soil, will unfold to industry the certain road to competence. To those hardy soldiers who are actuated by the spirit of adventure, the fisheries will afford ample and profitable employment ; and the extensive and fertile regions of the west will yield a most happy asylum to those who, fond of domestic enjoyment, are seeking personal independence. Nor is it possible to conceive that any one of the U-nited States will prefer a national bankruptcy, and the dissolution of the union, to a compliance with the requisitions of Congress, and the payment of its just debts; so that the officers and soldiers may expect considerable assistance, in recommencing their civil occupations, from the sums due to them from the public, which must and will most inevitably be paid.

IN order to effect this desirable purpose, and to remove the prejudices which may have taken possession of the minds of any of the good people of the states, it is earnestly recommended to all the troops, that, with strong attachments to the union, they should carry with them into civil society the most conciliating dispositions; and that they should prove themselves not less virtuous and useful as citizens, than they have been persevering and victorious as soldiers. What though there should be some envious individuals, who are unwilling to pay the debt the public has contracted, or to yield the tribute due to merit; yet let such unworthy treatment produce no invective, or any instance of intemperate conduct; let it be remembered, that the unbiassed voice of the free citizens of the United States has promised the just reward, and given the merited applause ; let it be known and remembered, that the reputation of the federal armies is established beyond the reach of malevolence ; and let a consciousness of their achievements, and fame, still excite the men who composed them to honourable actions, under the persuasion, that the private virtues of economy, prudence, and industry, will not be less amiable in civil life, than the more splendid qualities of valour, perseverance, and enterprize were in the field. Every one may rest assured that much of the future happiness of the officers and men, will depend upon the wise and manly conduct which shall be adopted by them, when they are mingled with the great body of the community. And although the general has so frequently given it as his opinion, in the most public and explicit manner, that unless the principles of the federal government were properly supported, and the powers of the union increased, the honour, dignity, and justice of the nation, would be lost forever ; yet he cannot help repeating on this occasion so interesting a sentiment, and leaving it as his last injunction to every officer and every soldier who may view the subject in the same serious point of light, to add his best endeavours to those of his worthy fellow-citizens, towards effecting these great and valuable purposes, on which our very exist-ence as a nation so materially depends.

THE commander in chief conceives little is now wanting to enable the soldier to change the military character into that of a citizen, but that steady and decent tenor of behaviour, which has generally distin-guished not only the army under his imme-diate command, but the different detach-ments and separate armies, through the course of the war. From their good sense and prudence he anticipated the happiest con-sequences : and while he congratulates them on the glorious occasion which renders their services in the field no longer necessary, he wishes to express the strong obligations he feels himself under for the assistance he has received from every class, and in every in-stance. He presents his thanks, in the most serious and affectionate manner, to the gen-eral officers, as well for their counsel on ma-ny interesting occasions, as for their ardour in promoting the success of the plans he had

adopted ; to the commandants of regiments
and corps, and to the officers for their zeal
and attention in carrying his orders prompt-
ly into execution ; to the staff, for their alacrity and exactness in performing the duties
of their several departments ; and to the non-
commissioned officers and private soldiers,
for their extraordinary patience in suffering,
as well as their invincible fortitude in action.
To all the branches of the army the general
takes this last and solemn opportunity of
professing his inviolable attachment and
friendship : he wishes more than bare pro-
fessions were in his power, that he was really able to be useful to them all in future life.
He flatters himself, however, they will do
him the justice to believe, that whatever
could with propriety be attempted by him,
has been done. And being now to conclude
these his last public orders, to take his ultimate leave, in a short time, of the military
character, and to bid a final adieu to the armies he has so long had the honour to command, he can only again offer, in their behalf, his recommendations to their grateful
country, and his prayers to the God of armies. May ample justice be done them here,
and may the choicest of heaven's favours,

both here and hereafter, attend those, who, under the divine auspices, have secured innumerable blessings for others ! With these wishes, and this benediction, the commander in chief is about to retire from service. The curtain of separation will soon be drawn— and the military scene, to him, will be closed forever.

ANNAPOLIS, DEC. 23, 1783.

GENERAL *WASHINGTON* having informed Congress of his intention to resign the commission he had the honor to hold in their service, they resolved that it should be done in a public audience ; and appointed this day for the interesting scene. At a proper moment, Gen. WASHINGTON appeared, and addressed The President in the following words :—

" *MR. PRESIDENT,*

" THE great events on which my resignation depended, having at length taken place, I have now the honour of offering my sincere congratulations to Congress, and of presenting myself before them to surrender into their hands, the trust committed to me, and to claim the indulgence of retiring from the service of my country.

" HAPPY in the confirmation of our independence and sovereignty, and pleased with the opportunity afforded the United States of becoming a respectable nation, I resign with satisfaction the appointment I accepted with diffidence ; a diffidence in my abilities to accomplish so arduous a task, which, however, was superseded by a confidence in the rectitude of our cause, the support of the supreme power of the union, and the patronage of heaven.

" THE successful termination of the war has verified the most sanguine expectations, and my gratitude for the interposition of providence, and the assistance I have received from my countrymen, increases with every review of the momentous contest.

" WHILE I repeat my obligations to the army in general, I should do injustice to my own feelings not to acknowledge, in this place, the peculiar services, and distinguished merits of the persons who have been attached to my person during the war : it was impossible the choice of confidential officers to compose my family should have been more fortunate : permit me, sir, to recommend in particular those who have continued in the service to the present moment, as worthy of the favorable notice and patronage of Congress.

" I consider it as an indispensable duty to close this last solemn act of my official life, by commending the interests of our dearest country to the protection of Almighty God, and those who have the superintendence of them, to his holy keeping.

" HAVING now finished the work assigned me, I retire from the great theatre of action ; and bidding an affectionate farewel to
this august body, under whose orders I have
long acted, I here offer my commission, and
take my leave of all the employments of public life."

TO WHICH THE PRESIDENT RETURNED THE
FOLLOWING ANSWER :

" THE United States in Congress assembled, receive with emotions too affecting for
utterance, the solemn resignation of the authorities under which you have led their
troops with success, through a perilous and
doubtful war.

" CALLED upon by your country to defend its invaded rights, you accepted the sacred charge before it had formed alliances,
and whilst it was without friends or a government to support you.

" YOU have conducted the great military
contest with wisdom and fortitude, invaria-
bly regarding the rights of the civil power
through all disasters and changes : you have

by the love and confidence of your fellow citizens enabled them to display their martial genius, and transmit their fame to posterity ; you have persevered, till these United States, aided by a magnanimous king and nation, have been enabled, under a just providence, to close the war in freedom, safety and independence ; on which happy event we sincerely join you in congratulations.

" HAVING defended the standard of liberty in this new world—having taught a lesson useful to those who inflict, and to those who feel oppression, you retire from the great theatre of action, with the blessing of your fellow citizens, but the glory of your virtues will not terminate with your military command, it will continue to animate remotest ages. We feel with you, our obligations to the army in general, and will particularly charge ourselves with the interest of those confidential officers, who have attended your person to this affecting moment.

" WE join you in commending the interests of our dearest country to the protection of Almighty God, beseeching Him to dispose the hearts and minds of its citizens, to improve the opportunity afforded them, of becoming a happy and respectable nation ; and for you, we address to Him our earnest prayers, that a life so beloved may be fostered with all his care : that your days may be happy as they have been illustrious, and that he will finally give you that reward which this world cannot give."

[NEW-YORK, APRIL 30,-1789.

THIS day the great and illustrious *WASHINGTON*, the favorite son of liberty, and deliverer of his country, entered upon
the execution of the office of First Magistrate of the United States
of America ; to which important station he had been unanimously called by the united voice of the people.   The ceremony which
took place on this occasion was truly grand and pleasing, and every heart seemed anxious to teſtify the joy it felt on ſo memorable
an event.   His Excellency was eſcorted from his house by a troop
of light dragoons, and a legion under the command of col. *Lewis*,
attended by a committee of the senate and house of representatives, to Federal Hall, where he was formally received by both
houses of Congress, assembled in the Senate Chamber ; after which
he was conducted to the gallery in front of the hall, accompanied
by all the members, when the oath, prescribed by the Constitution, was administered to him by the Chancellor of the State, who
then ſaid,

LONG LIVE
GEORGE WASHINGTON,
PRESIDENT
OF THE UNITED STATES,

which was answered by an immense concourse of citizens, assembled on the occasion, by the loudest plaudit and acclamation, that
love and veneration ever inspired.   He then made the following
Speech

THE PRESIDENT's SPEECH.

FELLOW-CITIZENS OF THE SENATE, AND
OF THE HOUSE OF REPRESENTATIVES,

AMONG the vicissitudes incident to
life, no event could have filled me with greater anxieties than that of which the notifica-
tion was transmitted by your order, and re-

ceived on the 14th day of the present month.
On the one hand, I was summoned by my
country, whose voice I can never hear but
with veneration and love, from a retreat
which I had chosen with the fondest predilection, and, in my flattering hopes, with an
immutable decision, as the asylum of my declining years : a retreat which was rendered
every day more necessary as well as more
dear to me, by the addition of habit to inclination, and of frequent interruptions in my
health to the gradual waste committed on it
by time.   On the other hand, the magnitude
and difficulty of the trust to which the voice
of my country called me, being sufficient to
awaken in the wisest and most experienced
of her citizens, a distrustful scrutiny into his
qualifications, could not but overwhelm with
despondence one, who, inheriting inferiour
endowments from nature, and unpractised
in the duties of civil administration, ought
to be peculiarly conscious of his own deficien-
cies.   In this conflict of emotions, all I dare
aver is, that it has been my faithful study to
collect my duty from a just appreciation of
every circumstance by which it might be affected.   All I dare hope is, that if in executing this task I have been too much swayed by

a grateful remembrance of former instances, or by an affectionate sensibility to this transcendent proof of the confidence of my fellow-citizens ; and have thence too little consulted my incapacity as well as disinclination for the weighty and untried cares before me; my error will be palliated by the motives which misled me, and its consequences be judged by my country, with some share of the partiality in which they originated.

SUCH being the impressions under which I have, in obedience to the public summons, repaired to the present station, it would be peculiarly improper to omit in this first official act, my fervent supplications to that Almighty Being, who rules over the universe, who presides in the councils of nations, and whose providential aids can supply every human defect, that his benediction may consecrate to the liberties and happiness of the people of the United States, a government instituted by themselves for these essential purposes, and may enable every instrument employed in its administration, to execute with success, the functions allotted to his charge. In tendering this homage to the great author of every public and private good, I assure

H

myself that it expresses your sentiments not less than my own ; nor those of my fellow-citizens at large, less than either. No people can be bound to acknowledge and adore the invisible hand, which conducts the affairs of men, more than the people of the United States. Every step, by which they have advanced to the character of an independent nation, seems to have been distinguished by some token of providential agency. And in the important revolution just accomplished in the system of their united government, the tranquil deliberations and voluntary consent of so many distinct communities, from which the event has resulted, cannot be compared with the means by which most governments have been established, without some return of pious gratitude along with an humble anticipation of the future blessings which the past seem to presage. These reflections, arising out of the present crisis, have forced themselves too strongly on my mind to be suppressed. You will join with me, I trust, in thinking that there are none under the influence of which, the proceedings of a new and free government can more auspiciously commence.

BY the article establishing the executive
department, it is made the duty of the president " to recommend to your consideration,
such measures as he shall judge necessary
and expedient." The circumstances under
which I now meet you, will acquit me from
entering into that subject farther than to re-
fer you to the great constitutional charter
under which we are assembled ; and which,
in defining your powers, designates the objects to which your attention is to be given.
It will be more consistent with those circumstances, and far more congenial with the feelings which actuate me, to substitute in place
of a recommendation of particular measures,
the tribute that is due to the talents, the rectitude, and the patriotism which adorn the
characters selected to devise and adopt them.
In these honourable qualifications, I behold
the surest pledges, that as on one side, no local prejudices or attachments, no separate
views nor party animosities, will misdirect
the comprehensive and equal eye which ought
to watch over this great assemblage of communities and interests : so, on the other, that
the foundations of our national policy will
be laid in the pure and immutable principles

of private morality ; and the pre-eminence of a free government be exemplified by all the attributes which can win the affections of its citizens, and command the respect of the world.

I DWELL on this prospect with every satisfaction which an ardent love for my country can inspire ; since there is no truth more thoroughly established, than that there exits in the economy and course of nature, an indissoluble union between virtue and happiness—between duty and advantage, between the genuine maxims of an honest and magnanimous policy, and the solid rewards of public prosperity and felicity. Since we ought to be no less persuaded that the propitious smiles of heaven can never be expected on a nation that disregards the eternal rules of order and right, which heaven itself has ordained ; and since the preservation of the sacred fire of liberty, and the destiny of the republican model of government, are justly considered as DEEPLY, perhaps as FINALLY staked, on the experiment entrusted to the hands of the American people.

BESIDES the ordinary objects submitted to your care, it will remain with your judgment to decide how far an exercise of the occasional power delegated by the fifth article of the constitution is rendered expedient at the present juncture by the nature of objections which have been urged against the system, or by the degree of inquietude which has given birth to them. Instead of undertaking particular recommendations on this subject, in which I could be guided by no lights derived from official opportunities, I shall again give way to my intire confidence in your discernment and pursuit of the public good : for I assure myself, that whilst you carefully avoid every alteration which might endanger the benefits of an united and effective government, or which ought to await the future lessons of experience ; a reverence for the characteristic rights of freemen, and a regard for the public harmony, will sufficiently influence your deliberations on the question, how far the former can be more impregnably fortified, or the latter be safely and advantageously promoted.

TO the preceding observations I have one to add, which will be most properly addressed to the house of representatives. It concerns myself, and will therefore be as brief as possible. When I was first honoured with a call into the service of my country, then on the eve of an arduous struggle for its liberties, the light in which I contemplated my duty, required that I should renounce every pecuniary compensation. From this resolution I have in no instance departed. And being still under the impressions which produced it, I must decline, as inapplicable to myself, any share in the personal emoluments, which may be indispensably included in a permanent provision for the executive department ; and must accordingly pray that the pecuniary estimates for the station in which I am placed, may, during my continuation in it, be limited to such actual expenditures as the public good may be thought to require.

HAVING thus imparted to you my sentiments, as they have been awakened by the occasion which brings us together, I shall take my present leave ; but not without resorting once more to the benign parent of the human race, in humble supplication, that since he has been pleased to favour the American people with opportunities for deliberating in perfect tranquility, and dispositions for deciding with unparalleled unanimity on a form of government for the security of their union, and the advancement of their happiness ; so his divine blessing may be equally *conspicuous* in the enlarged views, the temperate consultations, and the wise measures on which the success of this government must depend.

GEORGE WASHINGTON.

ADDRESS
OF GEORGE WASHINGTON,

PRESIDENT OF THE UNITED STATES, TO HIS
FELLOW CITIZENS, ON DECLINING BEING
CONSIDERED A CANDIDATE FOR THEIR FU-
TURE SUFFRAGES.

FRIENDS AND FELLOW-CITIZENS,

THE period for a new election of a Citizen, to administer the executive government of the United States, being not far distant, and the time actually arrived, when
your thoughts must be employed in desig-
nating the person, who is to be cloathed
with that important trust, it appears to me
proper, especially as it may conduce to a
more distinct expression of the public voice,
that I should now apprise you of the resolution I have formed, to decline being considered among the number of those, out of
whom a choice is to be made.

I BEG you, at the same time, to do me
the justice to be assured, that this resolution
has not been taken, without a strict regard
to all the considerations appertaining to the
relation, which binds a dutiful citizen to his
country ; and that, in withdrawing the ten-

der of service which silence in my situation
might imply, I am influenced by no diminu-
tion of zeal for your future interest ; no deficiency of grateful respect for your past kindness : but am supported by a full conviction
that the step is compatible with both.

THE acceptance of, and continuance hitherto in the office to which your suffrages
have twice called me, have been a uniform
sacrifice of inclination to the opinion of duty, and to a deference for what appeared to
be your desire. I constantly hoped, that it
would have been much earlier in my power
consistently with motives, which I was not
at liberty to disregard, to return to that retirement, from which I had been reluctantly
drawn. The strength of my inclination to do
this, previous to the last election, had even
led to the preparation of an address to declare it to you ; but mature reflection on the
then perplexed and critical posture of affairs
with foreign nations, and the unanimous advice of persons intitled to my confidence, impelled me to abandon the idea.

I REJOICE, that the state of your concerns, external as well as internal, no longer

I

renders the pursuit of inclination incompatible with the sentiment of duty, or propriety : and am persuaded, whatever partiality
may be retained for my service, that in the
present circumstances of our country, you
will not disapprove my determination to
retire.

THE impressions with which I first un-
dertook the arduous trust, were explained
on the proper occasion.   In the discharge of
this trust, I will only say, that I have with
good intentions, contributed towards the organization and administration of the government, the best exertions of which a very fal-
lible judgment was capable.   Not unconscious, in the outset, of the inferiority of my
qualifications, experience in my own eyes,
perhaps still more in the eyes of others, has
strengthened the motives to diffidence of
myself : and every day the increasing weight
of years admonishes me more and more, that
the shade of retirement is as necessary to me
as it will be welcome.   Satisfied that if any
circumstances have given peculiar value to
my services, they were temporary, I have
the consolation to believe, that while choice

and prudence invite me to quit the political scene, patriotism does not forbid it.

IN looking forward to the moment, which is intended to terminate the career of my public life, my feelings do not permit me to suspend the deep acknowledgment of that debt of gratitude which I owe to my beloved country, for the many honours it has conferred upon me ; still more for the stedfast confidence with which it has supported me ; and for the opportunities I have thence enjoyed of manifesting my inviolable attachment, by services faithful and persevering, though in usefulness unequal to my zeal.— If benefits have resulted to our country from these services, let it always be remembered to our praise, and as an instructive example in our annals, that under circumstances in which the passions, agitated in every direction, were liable to mislead, amidst appearances sometimes dubious, vicissitudes of fortune, often discouraging in situations, in which not unfrequently want of success has countenanced the spirit of criticism—the constancy of your support was the essential prop of the efforts, and a guarantee of the plans by which they were effected. Pro-

foundly penetrated with this idea, I shall carry it with me to my grave, as a strong in-
citement to unceasing vows, that heaven
may continue to you the choicest tokens of
its beneficence—that your union and brotherly affection may be perpetual—that the free
constitution, which is the work of your
hands, may be sacredly maintained—that its
administration in every department may be
stamped with wisdom and virtue—that, in
fine, the happiness of the people of these
states, under the auspices of liberty, may be
made complete, by so careful a preservation
and so prudent a use of this blessing, as will
acquire to them the glory of recommending
it to the applause, the affection, and adoption
of every nation which is yet a stranger to it.

HERE, perhaps, I ought to stop. But solicitude for your welfare, which cannot end
but with my life, and the apprehension of
danger natural to that solicitude, urge me
on an occasion like the present, to offer to
your solemn contemplation, and to recommend to your frequent review, some sentiments, which are the result of much reflection, of no inconsiderable observation, and
which appear to me all-important to the per-

manency of your felicity as a people. These
will be offered to you with the more freedom, as you can only feel in them the disinterested warnings of a parting friend, who
can possibly have no personal motive to bias
his counsel. Nor can I forget, as an encouragement to it, your indulgent reception of
my sentiments on a former and not dissim-
ilar occasion.

INTERWOVEN as is the love of liberty with
every ligament of your hearts, no recommendation of mine is necessary to fortify or
confirm the attachment.

THE unity of government which consti-
tutes you one people, is also now dear to you.
It is justly so ; for it is a main pillar in the
edifice of your real independence, the support of your tranquility at home, your peace
abroad ; of your safety ; of your prosperity ;
of that very liberty which you so highly
prize. But, as it is easy to foresee, that
from different causes and from different
quarters, much pains will be taken, many
artifices employed, to weaken in your minds
the conviction of this truth ; as this is the
point in your political fortress, against which

the batteries of internal and external enemies will be most constantly and actively,
(though often covertly and insidiously) directed, it is of infinite moment that you
should properly estimate the immense value
of your national union, to your collective
and individual happiness ; that you should
cherish a cordial, habitual, and immovable
attachment to it ; accustoming yourselves to
think and speak of it as of the palladium of
your political safety and prosperity, watching for its preservation with jealous anxiety;
discountenancing whatever may suggest even
a suspicion that it can in any event be abandoned ; and indignantly frowning upon the
first dawning of every attempt to alienate
any portion of our country from the rest,
or to enfeeble the sacred ties which now link
together the various parts.

For this you have every inducement of
sympathy and interest. Citizens, by birth or
choice, of a common country, that country
has a right to concentrate your affections.
The name of AMERICAN, which belongs to
you in your national capacity, must always
exalt the just pride of patriotism, more than
any appellation derived from local discrimi-

nations. With slight shades of difference,
you have the same religion, manners, habits
and political principles. You have in a common cause, fought and triumphed together ;
the independence and liberty you possess are
the work of joint councils, and joint efforts,
of common dangers, sufferings and suc-
cesses.

BUT these considerations however pow-
erfully they address themselves to your sensibility, are greatly outweighed by those
which apply more immediately to your interest. Here every portion of our country
finds the most commanding motives for carefully guarding and preserving the union of
the whole.

THE *North*, in an unrestrained intercourse
with the *South*, protected by the equal laws
of a common government, finds in the productions of the latter, great additional resources of maritime and commercial enter-
prise, and precious materials of manufactur-
ing industry. The *South* in the same intercourse, benefiting by the agency of the *North*,
sees its agriculture grow, and its commerce
expand. Turning partly into its own chan-

nels the seamen of the *North*, it finds its particular navigation invigorated—and, while it contributes, in different ways, to nourish and increase the general mass of the national navigation, it looks forward to the protection of a maritime strength, to which itself is unequally adapted. The *East* in a like intercourse with the *West*, already finds, and in the progressive improvement of interior communications, by land and water, will more and more find a valuable vent for the commodities which it brings from abroad, or manufactures at home. The *West* derives from the *East* supplies requisite to its growth and comfort ; and what is perhaps of still greater consequence, it must of necessity owe the *secure* enjoyment of indispensable *outlets* for its own productions to the weight, influence, and the future maritime strength of the atlantic side of the Union, directed by an indissoluble community of interests as *one nation*. Any other tenure by which the *West* can hold this essential advantage, whether derived from its own separate strength, or from an apostate and unnatural connection with any foreign power, must be intrinsically precarious.

WHILE then every part of our country thus feels an immediate and particular interest in union, all the parts combined cannot fail to find in the united mass of means and efforts, greater strength, greater resource, proportionably greater security, from external danger, a less frequent interruption of their peace by foreign nations ; and what is of inestimable value, they must derive from union an exemption from those broils and wars between themselves, which so frequently afflict neighbouring countries, not tied together by the same government ; which their own rivalships alone would be sufficient to produce, but which opposite foreign alliances, attachments and intrigues, would stimulate and imbitter. Hence, likewise, they will avoid the necessity of those overgrown military establishments, which, under any form of government, are inauspicious to liberty, and which are to be regarded as particularly hostile to republican liberty : in this sense it-is, that your union ought to be considered as a main prop of your liberty, and that the love of the one ought to endear to you the preservation of the other.

K

THESE considerations speak a persuasive language to every reflecting and virtuous mind, and exhibit the continuance of the UNION as a primary object of a patriotic desire. Is there a doubt, whether a common government can embrace so large a sphere ? —let experience solve it. To listen to mere speculation, in such a case, were criminal. We are authorized to hope that a proper organization of the whole, with the auxiliary agency of governments for the respective sub-divisions, will afford a happy issue to the experiment. It is well worth a fair and full experiment. With such powerful and obvious motives to union, affecting all parts of our country, while experiment shall not have demonstrated its impracticability, there will always be reason to distrust the patriotism of those, who, in any quarter, **may** endeavour to weaken its hands.

IN contemplating the causes which may disturb our union, it occurs as matter of serious concern, that any ground should be furnished for characterising parties, by *geographical* discriminations—*Northern* and *Southern*—*Atlantic* and *Western* ; whence designing men may endeavour to excite a belief,

that there is a real difference of local interests and views.   One of the expedients of
party, to acquire influence within particular
districts, is to misrepresent the opinions and
aims of other districts.   You cannot shield
yourselves too much against the jealousies
and heart-burnings which spring from these
misrepresentations : they tend to render
alien to each other, those who ought to be
bound together by fraternal affection.—The
inhabitants of our western country have
lately had a useful lesson on this head : they
have seen, in the negotiation by the executive, and in the unanimous ratification by
the senate, of the treaty with Spain, and in
the universal satisfaction at that event,
throughout the United States, a decisive
proof how unfounded were the suspicions
propogated among them, of a policy in the
general government, and in the atlantic states,
unfriendly to their interests, in regard to the
Missisippi ; they have been witnesses to the
formation of two treaties, that with Great-
Britain, and that with Spain, which secure to
them every thing they could desire, in respect
to our foreign relations, towards confirming
their prosperity.   Will it not be their wisdom to rely for the preservation of these ad-

vantages on the union by which they were procured ? Will they not henceforth be deaf to those advisers, if such they are, who would sever them from their brethren, and connect them with aliens ?

TO the efficacy and permanency of your union, a government for the whole is indispensable. No alliances, however strict, between the parts, can be an adequate substitute ; they will inevitably experience the infractions and interruptions which all alliances, in all times, have experienced. Sensible of this momentous truth, you have improved upon your first essay, by the adoption of a constitution of government better calculated than your former for an intimate union, and for the efficacious management of your common concerns. This government, the offspring of your own choice, uninfluenced and unawed, adopted upon full investigation, and mature deliberation, completely free in its principles, in the distribution of its powers, uniting security with energy, and containing, within itself, a provision for its own amendment, has a just claim to your confidence, and your support. Respect for its authority, compliance with its laws, acquies-

cence in its measures, are duties enjoined by
the fundamental maxims of true liberty.—
The basis of our political systems is the right
of the people to make and to alter their con-
stitutions of government.　But, the constitution which at any time exists, 'till changed
by an explicit and authentic act of the whole
people, is sacred and obligatory upon all. The
very idea of the power and the right of the
people to establish government, pre-suppose
the duty of every individual to obey the established government.

ALL obstructions to the execution of the
laws, all combinations and associations, under whatever plausible character, with the
real character to direct, controul, counteract,
or awe the regular deliberation and action of
the constituted authorities, are destructive of
this fundamental principle, and of fatal tendency.　They serve to organize faction, to
give it an artificial and extraordinary force,
to put in the place of the delegated will of
the nation, the will of a party, often a small,
but artful and enterprising minority of the
community ; and, according to the alternate
triumphs of different parties, to make the
public administration the mirror of the ill-

concerted and incongruous projects of faction, rather than the organ of consistent and wholesome plans, digested by common councils, and modified by mutual interests.

HOWEVER combinations or associations of the above description may now and then answer popular ends, they are likely in the course of time and things, to become potent engines, by which cunning, ambitious, and unprincipled men, will be enabled to subvert the power of the people, and to usurp for themselves the reins of government; destroying afterwards the very engines which have lifted them to unjust dominion.

TOWARDS the preservation of your government, and the permanency of your present happy state, it is requisite, not only that you steadily discountenance irregular opposition to its acknowledged authority, but also that you resist with care, the spirit of innovation upon its principles, however specious the pretexts. One method of assault may be to effect, in the forms of the constitution, alterations which will impair the energy of the system, and thus to undermine what cannot be directly overthrown. In all

the changes to which you may be invited,
remember that time and habit are at least as
necessary to fix the true character of government, as of other human institutions—that
experience is the surest standard, by which
to test the real tendency of the existing constitution of a country—that facility in changes upon the credit of mere hypothesis and
opinion, exposes to perpetual change, from
the endless variety of hypothesis and opinion ; and remember, especially, that for the
efficient management of your common interest, in a country so extensive as ours, a government of as much vigor as is consistent
with the perfect security of liberty, is indispensable.   Liberty itself will find in such a
government, with powers properly distribut-
ed and adjusted, its surest guardian.   It is,
indeed, little else than a name, where the
government is too feeble to withstand the
enterprises of faction, to confine each member of the society within the limits prescribed
by the laws, and to maintain all in the secure and tranquil enjoyment of the rights of
person and property.

    I HAVE already intimated to you, the dan-
ger of parties in the state, with particular re-

ference to the founding of them on geograph‑
ical discrimination.   Let me now take a
more comprehensive view, and warn you, in
the most solemn manner, against the bane‑
ful effects of the spirit of party, generally.

THIS spirit, unfortunately, is inseparable
from our nature, having its root in the
strongest passions of the human mind.   It
exists under different shapes in all govern‑
ments—more or less stifled, controuled, or
repressed ; but in those of the popular form,
it is seen in its greatest rankness, and is tru‑
ly their worst enemy.

THE alternate domination of one faction
over another, sharpened by the spirit of re‑
venge, natural to party dissension, which in
different ages and countries has perpetrated
the most horrid enormities, is itself a fright‑
ful despotism ; but this leads at length to a
more formal and permanent despotism.—
The disorders and miseries which result, grad‑
ually incline the minds of men to seek secu‑
rity and repose in the absolute power of an
individual ; and sooner or later the chief of
some prevailing faction, more able or more
fortunate than his competitors, turns this

disposition to the purposes of his own elevation, on the ruins of public liberty.

WITHOUT looking forward to an extremity of this kind (which nevertheless ought
not to be intirely out of sight) the common
and continual mischiefs of the spirit of party,
are sufficient to make it the interest and duty of a wise people to discourage and re-
strain it.

IT serves always to distract the public
councils, and enfeeble the public administration. It agitates the community with ill-
founded jealousies, and false alarms ; kindles
the animosity of one part against another,
foments occasionally riot and insurrection.
It opens the door to foreign influence and
corruption, which find a facilitated access to
the government itself through the channels
of party passions.   Thus the policy and will
of one country are subjected to the policy
and will of another.

THERE is an opinion, that parties in free
countries are useful checks upon the administration of the government, and serve to keep
alive the spirit of liberty.   This, within certain limits, is probably true, and in govern-

L

ments of a monarchial cast, patriotism may look with indulgence, if not with favour upon the spirit of party. But in those of the popular character, in governments purely elective, it is a spirit not to be encouraged. From their natural tendency it is certain there will always be enough of that spirit for every salutary purpose. And there being constant danger of excess, the effort ought to be by force of public opinion, to mitigate and assuage it. A fire not to be quenched; it demands uniform vigilance to prevent its bursting into a flame, lest, instead of warming, it should consume.

IT is important likewise, that the habits of thinking in a free country, should inspire caution in those entrusted with its administration, to confine themselves within their respective constitutional spheres, avoiding in the exercise of the powers of one department to encroach upon another. The spirit of encroachment tends to consolidate the powers of all the departments in one, and thus to create, whatever the form of government, a real despotism. A just estimate of that love of power, and proneness to abuse it, which predominates in the human heart is sufficient to satisfy us of the truth of this position. The necessity of reciprocal checks in the exercise of the political power, by dividing and distributing it into different depositories, and constituting each the guardian of the public weal against invasions by the others, has been evinced by experiments ancient and modern ; some of them in our country, and under our own eyes. To preserve them must be as necessary as to institute them. If, in the opinion of the people, the distribution or modification of the constitutional powers be, in any particular, wrong, let it be corrected by an amendment in the way, which the constitution designates —but let there be no change by usurpation ; for though this, in one instance, may be the instrument of good, it is the customary weapon by which free governments are destroyed.—The precedent must always greatly overbalance, in permanent evil, any partial or transient benefit which the use can at any time yield.

OF all the dispositions and habits which lead to political prosperity, religion and morality are indispensable supports. In vain would that man claim the tribute of patriotism, who would labour to subvert these great pillars of human happiness, these firmest props of the duties of men and citizens. The mere politician, equally with the pious man, ought to respect and to cherish them. —A volume could not trace all their connections with private and public felicity. Let it simply be asked where is the security for property, for reputation, for life, if the sense of religious obligation desert the oaths which are the instruments of investigation in courts of justice ?—And let us with caution indulge the supposition, that morality can be maintained without religion. Whatever may be conceded of the influence of refined education on minds of peculiar structure ; reason and experience both forbid us to expect that national morality can prevail in exclusion of religious principle.

IT is substantially true, that virtue or morality is a necessary spring of popular government. The rule indeed extends with more or less force to every species of free government. Who that is a sincere friend to it can look with indifference upon attempts to shake the foundation of the fabric ?

PROMOTE then as an object of primary importance, institutions for the general diffusion of knowledge. In proportion as the structure of a government gives force to public opinion, it is essential that public opinion should be enlightened.

AS a very important source of strength and security, cherish public credit. One method of preserving it, is to use it as sparingly as possible; avoiding occasions of expence, by cultivating peace, but remembering also, that timely disbursements, to prepare for dangers, frequently prevent much greater disbursements to repel it : avoiding likewise the accumulation of debt, not only by shunning occasions of expence, but by vigorous exertions in time of peace to discharge the debts, which unavoidable wars may have occasioned, not ungenerously throwing upon posterity the burthen which we ourselves ought to bear. The execution of these maxims belongs to your representatives ; but it is necessary that public opinion should co-operate. To facilitate to them the performance of their duty, it is essential that you should practically bear in mind that towards the payment of debts there must be revenue ; that to have revenue there must be taxes ; and none can be devised which are not more or less inconvenient and unpleasant ; that the intrinsic embarrassment inseparable from the selection of the proper objects (which is always a choice of difficulties) ought to be a decisive motive for a candid construction of the conduct of the government in making it, and for a spirit of acquiescence in the measures for obtaining revenue which the public exigencies may at any time dictate.

OBSERVE good faith and justice towards all nations ; cultivate peace and harmony with all—religion and morality enjoin this conduct ; and can it be, that good policy does not equally enjoin it? It will be worthy of a free, enlightened, and (at no distant period) a great nation, to give to mankind the magnanimous and novel example of a people always guided by an exalted justice and benevolence. Who can doubt that in the course of time and things, the fruits of such a plan would richly repay any temporary advantages which might be lost by a steady adherence to it? Can it be, that providence has not connected the permanent felicity of a nation with virtue? The experiment, at least, is recommended by every sentiment which ennobles human nature. Alas! is it render-ed impossible by its vices?

IN the execution of such a plan, nothing is more essential than that permanent, invet-erate antipathies against particular nations, and passionate attachments for others, should be excluded; and that in the place of them, just and amicable feelings towards all should be cultivated. The nation which indulges towards another an habitual hatred, or an habitual fondness, is in some degree a slave. It is a slave to its animosity, or to its affec-tion, either of which is sufficient to lead it astray from its duty and its interest. Anti-pathy in one nation against another, disposes each more readily to offer insult and injury, to lay hold of slight causes of umbrage, and to be haughty and intractable when accident-al or trifling occasions of dispute occur.

HENCE frequent collisions, obstinate, en-venomed and bloody contests. The nation, prompted by ill will and resentment, some-times impels to war the government, contra-ry to the best calculations of policy. The

government sometimes participates in the national propensity, and adopts, through passion, what reason would reject; at other
times, it makes the animosity of the nation
subservient to projects of hostility, instigated
by pride, ambition, and other sinister and
pernicious motives. The peace, often, sometimes, perhaps, the liberty, of nations has
been the victim.

so, likewise, a passionate attachment of
one nation for another, produces a variety
of evils. Sympathy for the favourite nation,
facilitating the illusion of an imaginary common interest, in cases where no real common interest exists, and infusing into one the
enmities of the other, betrays the former into a participation in the quarrels and wars
of the latter, without adequate inducement
or justification. It leads also to concessions
to the favourite nation, of privileges denied
to others, which is apt, doubly, to injure the
nation making the concessions ; by unneces-
sarily parting with what ought to have been
retained ; and by exciting jealousy, ill will,
and a disposition to retaliate, in the parties
from whom equal privileges are withheld :
and it gives to ambitious, corrupted, or de-

luded citizens (who devote themselves to the favourite nation) facility to betray, or sacrifice the interests of their own country, without odium, sometimes even with popularity; gilding with the appearances of a virtuous sense of obligation a commendable deference for public opinion, or a laudable zeal for public good, the base or foolish compliances of ambition, corruption, or infatuation.

AS avenues to foreign influence in innumerable ways, such attachments are particularly alarming to the truly enlightened and independent patriot. How many opportunities do they afford to tamper with domestic factions, to practise the arts of seduction, to mislead public opinion, to influence or awe the public councils ; such an attachment of a small or weak, towards a great and powerful nation, dooms the former to be the satellite of the latter.

AGAINST the insidious wiles of foreign influence (I conjure you to believe me, fellow citizens) the jealousy of a free people ought to be *conftantly* awake ; since history and experience prove that foreign influence is one of the most baneful foes of republican gov-

ernment. But that jealousy to be useful
must be impartial ; else it becomes the instrument of the very influence to be avoided, instead of a defence against it. Excessive partiality for one foreign nation, and excessive
dislike of another, cause those, whom
they actuate, to see danger only on one side,
and serve to veil and even second the arts of
influence on the other. Real patriots, who
may resist the intrigues of the favourite, are
liable to become suspected and odious ; while
its tools and dupes usurp the applause and
confidence of the people, to surrender their
interests.

THE great rule of conduct for us in regard to foreign nations, is, in extending our
commercial relations, to have with them as
little *political* connection as possible. So far
as we have already formed engagements, let
them be fulfilled with perfect good faith.—
Here let us stop.

EUROPE has a set of primary interests,
which to us have none, or a very remote relation. Hence she must be engaged in frequent controversies, the causes of which are
essentially foreign to our concerns. Hence,

therefore, it must be unwise in us to impli-
cate ourselves, by artificial ties, in the ordinary vicissitudes of her politics, or the ordinary combinations and collisions of her
friendships, or enmities.

OUR detached and distant situation, in-
vites and enables us to pursue a different
course. If we remain one people, under an
efficient government, the period is not far
off, when we may defy material injury from
external annoyance ; when we may take
such an attitude as will cause the neutrality,
we may at any time resolve upon, to be scru-
pulously respected ; when belligerent nations,
under the impossibility of making acquisitions upon us, will not lightly hazard the
giving us provocation ; when we may choose
peace or war, as our interest, guided by justice, shall counsel.

WHY forego the advantages of so peculiar
a situation ? why quit our own, to stand
upon foreign ground ? why, by interweav-
ing our destiny with that of any part of
Europe, entangle our peace and prosperity in
the toils of European ambition, rivalship, interest, humour or caprice ?

IT is our true policy to steer clear of permanent alliances, with any portion of the foreign world ; so far, I mean, as we are now at liberty to do it ; for let me not be understood as capable of patronizing infidelity to existing engagements.   I hold the maxim no less applicable to public than to private affairs, that honesty is always the best policy.   I repeat it, therefore, let those engagements be observed in their genuine sense.   But, in my opinion, it is unnecessary, and would be unwise to extend them.

TAKING care always to keep ourselves, by suitable establishments, in a respectable defensive posture, we may safely trust to temporary alliances for extraordinary emergencies.

HARMONY, liberal intercourse with all nations, are recommended by policy, humanity and interest.   But even our commercial policy should hold an equal and impartial hand ; neither seeking or granting exclusive favours or preferences—consulting the natural course of things ; diffusing and diversifying, by gentle means, the streams of commerce, but forcing nothing ; establishing,

with the powers so disposed,in order to give
trade a stable course, to define the rights of
our merchants, and to enable the government to support them ; conventional rules
of intercourse, the best that present circumstances and mutual opinion will permit, but
temporary, and liable to be from time to
time abandoned or varied, as experience and
circumstances shall dictate ; constantly keeping in view, that it is folly in one nation to
look for disinterested favours from another ;
that it must pay, with a portion of its independence, for whatever it may accept under
that character ; that by such acceptance, it
may place itself in the condition of having
given equivalents for nominal favours, and
yet of being reproached with ingratitude for
not giving more. There can be no greater
error than to expect, or calculate, upon real
favours from nation to nation. It is an illusion which experience must cure, which a
just pride ought to discard.

IN offering to you, my countrymen, these
counsels of an old and affectionate friend, I dare
not hope they will make the strong and lasting impression I could wish—that they will
controul the usual current of the passions, or

prevent our nation from running the course which has hitherto marked the destiny of nations : but, if I may even flatter myself, that they may be productive of some partial benefit, some occsasional good ; that they may now and then recur to moderate the fury of party spirit, to warn against the mischiefs of foreign intrigue, to guard against the impostures of pretended patriotism ; this hope will be a full recompence for the solicitude for your welfare, by which they have been dictated.

HOW far, in the discharge of my official duties, I have been guided by the principles which have been delineated, the public records and other evidences of my conduct must witness to you and to the world. To myself, the assurance of my own conscience is, that I have at least believed myself to be guided by them.

IN relation to the still subsisting war in Europe, my proclamation of the 22d April, 1793, is the index to my plan. Sanctioned by your approving voice, and by that of your representatives, in both houses of Congress, the spirit of that measure has continu-

ally governed me ; uninfluenced by any attempts to deter or divert me from it.

AFTER deliberate examination, with the
aid of the best lights I could obtain, I was
well satisfied that our country, under all the
circumstances of the case,had a right to take,
and was bound in duty and interest to take,
a neutral position. Having taken it, I determined, as far as should depend on me, to
maintain it, with moderation.

THE considerations which respect the
right to hold this conduct, it is not necessary
on this occason to detail. I will only observe, that according to my understanding
of the matter, that right, so far from being
denied by any of the belligerent powers, has
been virtually admitted by all.

THE duty of holding a neutral conduct
may be inferred, without any thing more,
from the obligation which justice and humanity impose on every nation, in cases in
which it is free to act, to maintain inviolate
the relations of peace and amity towards
other nations.

THE inducements of interest for observing that conduct, will be best referred to your own reflections and experience. With me, a predominant motive has been to endeavour to gain time to our country to settle and mature its yet recent institutions, and to progress without interruption, to that degree of strength and consistency, which is necessary to give it, humanly speaking, the command of its own fortunes.

THOUGH in reviewing the incidents of my administration, I am unconscious of intentional error, I am, nevertheless, too sensible of my defects not to think it probable that I may have committed many errors. Whatever they may be, I fervently beseech the Almighty to avert or mitigate the evils, to which they may tend. I shall also carry with me the hope that my country will never cease to view them with indulgence; and that, after forty-five years of my life dedicated to its service, with an upright zeal, the faults of incompetent abilities will be consigned to oblivion, as myself must soon be to the mansions of rest.

RELYING on its kindness in this as in other things, and actuated by that fervent love towards it, which is so natural to a man who views in it the native soil of himself and his progenitors for several generations, I anticipate with pleasing expectation that retreat, in which I promise myself to realize, without alloy, the sweet enjoyment of partaking, in the midst of my fellow-citizens, the benign influence of good laws under a free government—the ever favorite object of my heart, and the happy reward, as I trust, of our mutual cares, labours and dangers.

G. WASHINGTON.

UNITED STATES, SEPT. 17, 1796.

N

GEN. *WASHINGTON's LETTER,*

ON HIS ACCEPTING THE COMMAND OF THE
AMERICAN ARMY IN 1798.

Mount Vernon, July 13, 1798.

DEAR SIR,

I HAD the honour, on the evening of the 11th instant, to receive from the hand of the secretary of war, your favour of the 7th, announcing that you had, with the advice and consent of the senate, appointed me " Lieutenant General and Commander in Chief of all the armies raised, or to be raised, for the service of the United States."

I CANNOT express how greatly affected I am at this new proof of public confidence, and the highly flattering manner in which you have been pleased to make the communication ; at the same time, I must not conceal from you my earnest wish, that the choice had fallen upon a man less declined in years, and better qualified to encounter the usual vicissitudes of war.

YOU know, sir, what calculation I had made relative to the probable course of events, on my retiring from office, and the determination I had consoled myself with, of

closing the remnant of my days in my present peaceful abode ; you will, therefore, be
at no loss to conceive and appreciate the sensations I must have experienced, to bring
my mind to any conclusion, that would
pledge me, at so late a period of life, to leave
scenes I sincerely love, to enter upon the
boundless field of public action, incessant
trouble, and high responsibility.

IT was not possible for me to remain ig-
norant of, or indifferent to, recent transactions.

THE conduct of the Directory of France
towards our country ; their insidious hostility to its government ; their various practices
to withdraw the affections of the people from
it ; the evident tendency of their acts, and
those of their agents, to countenance and invigorate opposition ; their disregard of solemn treaties and the laws of nations ; their
war upon our defenceless commerce ; their
treatment of our ministers of peace, and
their demands, amounting to tribute, could
not fail to excite in me corresponding sentiments, with those my countrymen have so
generally expressed in their affectionate ad-

dresses to you.—Believe me, sir, no one can more cordially approve of the wise and prudent measures of your administration. They ought to inspire universal confidence, and will, no doubt, combined with the state of things, call from Congress such laws and means as will enable you to meet the full force and extent of the crisis.

SATISFIED thereof, that you have sincerely wished and endeavoured to avert war, and exhausted, to the last drop, the cup of reconciliation, we can with pure hearts appeal to heaven for the justice of our cause ; and may confidently trust the final result to that kind providencce who has heretofore, and so often, signally favoured the people of these United States.

THINKING in this manner, and feeling how incumbent it is upon every person, of every description, to contribute at all times to his country's welfare, especially in a moment like the present, when every thing we hold dear and sacred is so seriously threatened ; I have finally determined to accept the commission of commander in chief of the armies of the United States ; with this reserve only, that I shall not be called into the field until the army is in a situation to require my presence, or it becomes indispensable by the urgency of circumstances.

IN making this reservation, I beg it may be understood, that I do not mean to withhold any assistance to arrange and organize the army, which you think I can afford. I take the liberty also to mention, that I must decline having my acceptance considered as drawing after it any immediate charge upon the public; or that I can receive any emoluments annexed to the appointment, before entering into a situation to incur expence.

THE secretary of war being anxious to return to the seat of government, I have detained him no longer than was necessary to a full communication upon the several points he had in charge.

WITH very great respect and consideration, I have the honour to be, dear sir, your most obedient, humble servant,

G. WASHINGTON,

JOHN ADAMS,
Prefident of the United States.

𝔄𝔭𝔭𝔢𝔫𝔡𝔦𝔵.

CONGRESS OF THE UNITED STATES,
House of Representatives, Dec. 18, 1799.

IMMEDIATELY after the journals were read, General MARSHALL came into the house of representatives, apparently much agitated, and said,

MR. SPEAKER,

INFORMATION has just been received, that our illustrious fellow-citizen, the commander in chief of the American army, and the late president of the United States, is no more. Though this distressing intelligence is not certain, there is too much reason to believe its truth.

AFTER receiving information of a national calamity so heavy, and so afflicting, the house of representatives can be but ill fitted for public business. I move you, therefore, that we adjourn.

The house immediately adjourned.

THURSDAY, DEC. 19.

The following Message was received from THE
PRESIDENT *of the United States.*

Gentlemen of the House of Representatives,

THE letter herewith transmitted will inform you, that it has pleased Divine Providence to remove from this life, our excellent
fellow-citizen, GEORGE WASHINGTON,
by the purity of his character, and a long series of services to his country, rendered illustrious through the world.   It remains for an
affectionate and grateful people, in whose
hearts he can never die, to pay suitable honour to his memory.

JOHN ADAMS.

" Mount Vernon, Dec. 16, 1799.

" SIR,

" IT is with inexpressible grief that I have
to announce to you the death of the great and
good Gen. WASHINGTON.   He died last even-
ning, between 10 and 11 o'clock, after a short
illness of about twenty-four hours.   His disorder was an inflammatory sore throat,
which proceeded from a cold, of which he
made but little complaint on Friday.   On

Saturday morning about three o'clock, he became ill. Dr. DICK attended him in the morning, and Dr. CRAIK, of Alexandria, and Dr. BROWN, of Port Tobacco, were soon after called in. Every medical assistance was offered, but without the desired effect. His last scene corresponded with the whole tenor of his life. Not a groan, nor a complaint, escaped him, though in extreme distress.— With perfect resignation, and a full possession of his reason, he closed his well-spent life. I have the honor to be, &c.

"*TOBIAS LEAR.*

" *The President of the United States.*"

GEN. MARSHALL, with deep sorrow on his countenance, and in a pathetic tone of voice, thus addressed the house :—

MR. SPEAKER,

THE melancholy event which was yesterday announced with doubt, has been rendered but too certain. Our WASHINGTON is no more !—The hero, the sage, and the patriot of America—the man on whom in times of danger, every eye was turned, and all

hopes were placed, lives now, only in his
own great actions, and in the hearts of an affectionate and affected people.

IF, sir, it had not been usual, openly to
testify respect for the memory of those
whom heaven had selected as its instruments,
for dispensing good to man : yet, such has
been the uncommon worth, and such the extraordinary incidents which have marked the
life of him whose loss we all deplore, that
the whole American nation, impelled by the
same feelings, would call with one voice for
a public manifestation of that sorrow which
is so deep and so universal.

MORE than any other individual, and as
much as to one individual was possible, has
he contributed to found this our wide
spreading empire, and to give to the western
world its independence and its freedom. Having effected the great object for which he was
placed at the head of our armies, we have
seen him convert the sword into the ploughshare, and voluntarily sink the soldier in the
citizen.

WHEN the debility of our federal system
had become manifest, and the bonds which
connected the parts of this vast continent
were dissolving, we had seen him the chief
of those patriots who formed for us a constitution, which, by preserving the union, will,
I trust, substantiate and perpetuate those
blessings our revolution had promised to bestow.

IN obedience to the general voice of his
country, calling on him to preside over a
great people, we have seen him once more
quit the retirement he loved, and in a season
more stormy and tempestuous than war itself, with calm and wise determination pursue the true interests of the nation, and contribute, more than any other could contribute, to
the establishment of that system of policy
which will, I trust, yet preserve our peace,
our honour, and our independence. Having been twice unanimously chosen the chief
magistrate of a free people, we see him, at a
time when his re-election with the universal
suffrage could not have been doubted, afford-
ing the world a rare instance of moderation,
by withdrawing from his high station to the
peaceful walks of private life.

HOWEVER public confidence may change, and the public affections fluctuate with respect to others, yet, with respect to him, they have, in war and in peace, in public and in private life, been as steady as his own firm mind, and as constant as his own exalted virtues.

LET us then, Mr. Speaker, pay the last tribute of respect and affection to our departed friend. Let the grand council of the nation display those sentiments which the nation feels.

FOR this purpose, I hold in my hand some resolutions which I will take the liberty to offer to the house :

" RESOLVED, that this house will wait on the president of the United States, in condolence of this mournful event :

" RESOLVED, that the speaker's chair be shrouded with black, and that the members and officers of the house wear black during the session :

" RESOLVED, that a committee, in conjunction with one from the senate, be appointed to consider on the most suitable manner of paying honour to the memory of the man, first in war, first in peace, and first in the hearts of his country :

" RESOLVED, that this house, when it adjourn, do adjourn to Monday."

THESE resolutions were unanimously agreed to. Sixteen members were appointed on the third resolution.

———————

GENERALS MARSHALL and SMITH, having waited on the president to know when he would be ready to receive the house—the president named one o'clock this day. The house accordingly waited on him, when the speaker thus addressed the president :

SIR,

THE house of representatives, penetrated with a sense of the irreparable loss sustained by the nation, by the death of that great and good man, the illustrious and beloved WASHINGTON, wait on you, Sir, to express their condolence on this melancholy and distressing event.

To which the President replied.

Gentlemen of the House of Representatives,

I RECEIVE with the greatest respect and affection, the condolence of the house of representatives, on the melancholy and afflicting event in the death of the most illustrious and beloved personage which this country ever produced. I sympathize with you—with the nation, and with good men, through the world, in the irreparable loss sustained by us all.

JOHN ADAMS.

PHILADELPHIA, DEC. 23, 1799.

THE senate of the United States, this day, sent the following letter of condolence to the president, by a committe of its members, to which he returned the annexed answer.

TO THE PRESIDENT OF THE UNITED STATES.

THE senate of the United States respectfully take leave, sir, to express to you their deep regret for the loss their country sus-

tains in the death of GENERAL GEORGE
WASHINGTON.

THIS event, so distressing to all our fellow citizens, must be peculiarly heavy on
you, who have long been associated with
him in deeds of patriotism. Permit us, sir,
to mingle our tears with yours : on this occasion it is manly to weep. To lose such a
man at such a crisis is no common calamity
to the world : our country mourns her father. The Almighty Disposer of human events
has taken from us our greatest benefactor
and ornament. It becomes us to submit
with reverence to him, who " maketh darkness his pavilion."

WITH patriotic pride we review the life
of our WASHINGTON, and compare him
with those of other countries who have been
pre-eminent in fame. Ancient and modern
names are diminished before him. Greatness and guilt have too often been allied; but
his fame is whiter than it is brilliant. The
destroyers of nations stood abashed at the
majesty of his virtues. It reproved the in-
temperance of their ambition, and darkened
the splendour of victory. The scene is closed,

and we are no longer anxious lest misfortune should sully his glory ; he has travelled to the end of his journey, and carried with him an increasing weight of glory ; he has deposited it safely, where misfortune cannot tarnish it, where malice cannot blast it. Favoured of heaven, he departed without exhibiting the weaknes of humanity ; magnanimous in death, the darkness of the grave could not obscure his brightness.

SUCH was the man whom we deplore. Thanks to GOD, his glory is consummated ; WASHINGTON yet lives on earth in his spotless example—his spirit is in heaven.

LET his countrymen consecrate the memory of the heroic general, the patriotic statesman, and the virtuous sage : let them teach their children never to forget that the fruits of his labours, and his example, are their inheritance.

PRESIDENT's ANSWER.

GENTLEMEN OF THE SENATE,

I RECEIVE with the most respectful and affectionate sentiments, in this impressive

address, the obliging expressions of your regret, for the loss our country has sustained,
in the death of her most esteemed, beloved,
and admired citizen.

IN the multitude of my thoughts and re-
collections on this melancholy event, you will
permit me only to say, that I have seen him
in the days of adversity, in some of the
scenes of his deepest distress and most trying
perplexities—I have also attended him in his
highest elevation and most prosperous felicity—with uniform admiration of his wisdom,
moderation and constancy.

AMONG all our original associates, in that
memorable league of the continent in 1774,
which first expressed the sovereign will of a
free nation in America, he was the only one
remaining in the general government. Although, with a constitution more enfeebled
than his, at an age when he thought it necessary to prepare for retirement, I feel myself alone, bereaved of my last brother—yet
I derive a strong consolation from the unanimous disposition, which appears in all ages
and classes, to mingle their sorrows with
mine, on this common calamity to the
world.　　　P

THE life of our WASHINGTON cannot suffer by a comparison with those of other countries, who have been most celebrated and exalted by fame. The attributes and decorations of royalty, could have only served to eclipse the majesty of those virtues which made him, from being a modest citizen, a more resplendent luminary. Misfortune, had he lived, could hereafter have sullied his glory only with those superficial minds, who, believing that characters and actions are marked by success alone, rarely deserve to enjoy it. Malice could never have blasted his honour, and envy made him a singular exception to her universal rule.

FOR himself he had lived enough, to life and to glory ; for his fellow-citizens, if their prayers could have been answered, he would have been immortal. For me, his departure is at a most unfortunate moment. Trusting, however, in the wise and righteous dominion of providence over the passions of men, and the results of their councils and actions, as well as over their lives, nothing remains for me, but humble resignation.

HIS example is now complete, and it will teach wisdom and virtue to magistrates, citi-zens, and men, not only in the present age, but in future generations, as long as our history shall be read. If a TRAJAN found a PLINY, a MARCUS AURELIUS can never want biographers, eulogists, or historians.

JOHN ADAMS.

IN the house of representatives, General MARSHALL made a report, in part, from the joint committee appointed to consider a suitable mode of commemorating the death of Gen. WASHINGTON.

HE reported the following resolutions :

Resolved by the senate and house of represen-tatives of the United States of America, in con-gress assembled, that a marble monument be erected, by the United States, in the capitol of the city of WASHINGTON, and that the family of General WASHINGTON be requested to permit his body to be deposited under it, and that the monument be so designed as to commemorate the great events of his military and political life.

And be it further resolved, that there be a funeral procession from Congress hall, to the German Lutheran church, in memory of GENERAL GEORGE WASHINGTON, on Thursday, the 26th inst. and that an oration be prepared at the request of Congress, to be delivered before both houses on that day ; and that the president of the senate, and speaker of the house of representatives, be desired to request one of the members of Congress to prepare and deliver the same.

And be it further resolved, that it be recommended to the people of the United States, to wear crape on their left arm, as mourning, for thirty days.

And be it further resolved, that the president be requested to direct a copy of these resolutions to be transmitted to Mrs. WASHINGTON, assuring her of the profound respect Congress will ever bear to her person and character, of their condolence on the late afflicting dispensation of providence, and entreating her assent to the interment of the remains of General WASHINGTON in the manner expressed in the first resolution.

And be it further resolved, that the president be requested to issue a proclamation, notifying to the people throughout the U-nited States, the recommendation contained in the third resolution.

THESE resolutions passed both houses unanimously.

DECEMBER 24.

THIS day, in the house of representatives, the speaker informed the house, that in conformity to the second resolution passed on Monday, Major-General LEE had been appointed, by the president of the senate, and the speaker of the house of representatives, to prepare and deliver the oration in honour of our late illustrious commander in chief, on Thursday next, which appointment he had been pleased to accept.

A MESSAGE was received from the president of the United States, notifying the house that he had agreed to the resolutions passed on Monday, in honour to the memory of GENERAL WASHINGTON, and depos-ited them among the rolls and records of the United States.

FUNERAL ORATION,

ON THE DEATH OF GENERAL *WASHINGTON*, PRO-
NOUNCED BEFORE BOTH HOUSES OF CONGRESS, ON
THE 26th DECEMBER. 1799:

BY MAJOR-GENERAL Henry Lee.

IN obedience to your will, I rise your
humble organ, with the hope of executing a
part of the system of public mourning which
you have been pleased to adopt, commemo-
rative of the death of the most illustrious
and most beloved personage this country has ever produced ; and which, while it
transmits to posterity your sense of the awful event, faintly represents your knowledge
of the consummate excellence you so cordially honour.

DESPERATE indeed is any attempt on
earth to meet correspondently this dispensation of heaven ; for while with pious resignation we submit to the will of an all-gra-
cious providence, we can never cease lamenting, in our finite view of omnipotent wisdom, the heart-rending privation for which
our nation weeps. When the civilized
world shakes to its centre ; when every mo-

ment gives birth to strange and momentous changes ; when our peaceful quarter of the globe, exempt as it happily has been from any share in the slaughter of the human race, may yet be compelled to abandon her pacific policy, and to risk the doleful casualities of war : what limit is there to the extent of our loss ?—none within the reach of my words to express ; none which your feelings will not disavow.

THE founder of our federate republic— our bulwark in war, our guide in peace, is no more ! oh that this were but questionable ! hope, the comforter of the wretched, would pour into our agonizing hearts its balmy dew. But, alas ! there is no hope for us ; our WASHINGTON is removed forever ! possessing the stoutest frame, and purest mind, he had passed nearly to his sixtyeighth year, in the enjoyment of high health, when, habituated by his care of us to neglect himself, a slight cold, disregarded, became inconvenient on Friday, oppressive on Saturday, and, defying every medical interposition, before the morning of Sunday, put an end to the best of men. An end did I say ?—his fame survives ! bounded only by

the limits of the earth, and by the extent of
the human mind.   He survives in our hearts,
in the growing knowledge of our children,
in the affection of the good throughout the
world ; and when our monuments shall be
done away ; when nations now existing shall
be no more ; when even our young and far-
spreading empire shall have perished, still will
our WASHINGTON's glory unfaded shine,
and die not until love of virtue cease on
earth, or earth itself sinks into chaos.

HOW, my fellow citizens, shall I single to
your grateful hearts his pre-eminent worth !
where shall I begin in opening to your view
a character throughout sublime ? shall I speak
of his warlike achievements, all springing
from obedience to his country's will—all directed to his country's good ?

WILL you go with me to the banks of
the Monongahela, to see your youthful WASH-
INGTON, supporting, in the dismal hour of
Indian victory, the ill-fated BRADDOCK, and
saving, by his judgment, and by his valour,
the remains of a defeated army, pressed by
the conquering savage foe ? Or, when oppressed America, nobly resolving to risk her

all in defence of her violated rights, he was
elevated by the unanimous voice of Congress
to the command of her armies : will you follow him to the high grounds of Boston,
where to an undisciplined, courageous, and
virtuous yeomanry, his presence gave the
stability of system, and infused the invinci-
bility of love of country ; or shall I carry
you to the painful scenes of Long-Island,
York-Island and New-Jersey, when, combat-
ing superior and gallant armies, aided by
powerful fleets, and led by chiefs high in the
roll of fame, he stood the bulwark of our
safety ; undismayed by disaster ; unchanged
by change of fortune. Or will you view
him in the precarious fields of Trenton,
where deep gloom unnerving every arm,
reigned triumphant through our thinned,
worn down, unaided ranks ; himself unmoved.—Dreadful was the night. It was
about this time of winter—the storm raged—
the Delaware, rolling furiously with floating
ice, forbad the approach of man. WASH-
INGTON, self collected, viewed the tremend-
ous scene—his country called ; unappalled by
surrounding dangers, he passed to the hostile shore ; he fought ; he conquered. The
morning sun cheered the American world.

Our country rose on the event ; and her
dauntless chief, pursuing his blow, completed
in the lawns of Princeton, what his vast soul
had conceived on the shores of Delaware.

THENCE to the strong grounds of Morris-
town he led his small but gallant band ; and
through an eventful winter, by the high efforts of his genius, whose matchless force
was measurable only by the growth of difficulties, he held in check formidable hostile
legions, conducted by a chief experienced in
the art of war, and famed for his valour on
the ever memorable heights of Abraham,
where fell WOLFE, MONTCALM, and since,
our much lamented MONTGOMERY—all covered with glory. In this fortunate interval, produced by his masterly conduct, our fathers,
ourselves, animated by his resistless example,
rallied around our country's standard, and
continued to follow her beloved chief
through the various and trying scenes to
which the destinies of our union led.

WHO is there that has forgotten the vales
of Brandywine—the fields of Germantown
—or the plains of Monmouth ? every where
present, wants of every kind obstructing,

numerous and valiant armies encountering, himself a host, he assuaged our sufferings, limited our privations, and upheld our tottering republic. Shall I display to you the spread of the fire of his soul, by rehearsing the praises of the hero of Saratoga, and his much loved compeer of the Carolinas? no; our WASHINGTON wears not borrowed glory: to GATES—to GREENE, he gave without reserve the applause due to their eminent merit; and long may the chiefs of Saratoga, and of Eutaws, receive the grateful respect of a grateful people.

MOVING in his own orbit, he imparted heat and light to his most distant satellites; and combining the physical and moral force of all within his sphere, with irresistible weight he took his course, commiserating folly, disdaining vice, dismaying treason, and checking despondency; until the auspicious hour arrived, when, united with the intrepid forces of a potent and magnanimous ally, he brought to submission the since conqueror of India; thus finishing his long career of military glory with a lustre corresponding to his great name, and in this his last act of war, affixing the seal of fate to our nation's birth.

To the horrid din of battle sweet peace succeeded ; and our virtuous chief, mindful only of the common good, in a moment tempting personal aggrandizement, hushed the discontents of growing sedition ; and, surrendering his power into the hands from which he had received it, converted his sword into a ploughshare, teaching an admiring world that to be truly great, you must be truly good.

Was I to stop here, the picture would be incomplete, and the task imposed unfinished. Great as was our WASHINGTON in war, and as much as did that greatness contribute to produce the American republic, it is not in war alone his pre-eminence stands conspicuous : his various talents combining all the capacities of a statesman with those of a soldier, fitted him alike to guide the councils and the armies of our nation. Scarcely had he rested from his martial toils, while his invaluable parental advice was still sounding in our ears, when he who had been our shield and our sword, was called forth to act a less splendid but more important part.

POSSESSING a clear and penetrating mind, a strong and sound judgment, calmness and temper for deliberation, with invincible firmness and perseverance in resolutions maturely formed, drawing information from all, acting from himself, with incorruptible integrity and unvarying patriotism : his own superiority and the public confidence alike marked him as the man designed by heaven to lead in the great political, as well as military events, which have distinguished the era of his life.

THE finger of an over-ruling providence, pointing at WASHINGTON, was neither mistaken nor unobserved ; when, to realize the vast hopes to which our revolution had given birth, a change of political system became indispensable.

HOW novel, how grand the spectacle ! independent states stretched over an immense territory, and known only by common difficulty, clinging to their union as the rock of their safety, deciding by frank comparison of their relative condition, to rear on that

rock, under the guidance of reason, a common government through whose commanding protection, liberty aud order, with their
long train of blessings, should be safe to themselves, and the sure inheritance of their posterity.

THIS arduous task devolved on citizens
selected by the people, from knowledge of
their wisdom, and confidence in their virtue.
In this august assembly of sages and of patriots, WASHINGTON of course was found;
and, as if acknowledged to be most wise,
where all were wise, with one voice he was
declared their chief. How well he merited
this rare distinction, how faithful were the
labours of himself and his compatriots, the
work of their hands, and our union, strength
and prosperity, the fruits of that work, best
attest.

BUT to have essentially aided in presenting to his country this consummation of her
hopes, neither satisfied the claims of his fellow-citizens on his talents, nor those duties
which the possession of those talents imposed. Heaven had not infused into his
mind such an uncommon share of its ethe-

rial spirit to remain unemployed, nor bestowed on him his genius unaccompanied with
the corresponding duty of devoting it to the
common good. To have framed a constitution, was shewing only, without realizing,
the general happiness. This great work re-
mained to be done ; and America, stedfast
in her preference, with one voice summoned
her beloved WASHINGTON, unpractised
as he was in the duties of civil administration, to execute this last act in the completion of the national felicity. Obedient to
her call, he assumed the high office with that
self-distrust peculiar to his innate modesty,
the constant attendant of pre-eminent virtue.
What was the burst of joy through our anxious land on this exhilerating event is known
to us all. The aged, the young, the brave,
the fair, rivalled each other in demonstrations
of their gratitude ; and this high wrought,
delightful scene, was heightened in its effect,
by the singular contest between the zeal of
the bestowers and the avoidance of the re-
ceiver of the honors bestowed. Commenc-
ing his administration, what heart is not
charmed with the recollection of the pure
and wise principles announced by himself, as
the basis of his political life. He best un-

derstood the indissoluble union between virtue and happiness, between duty and advantage, between the genuine maxims of an honest and magnanimous policy, and the solid
rewards of public prosperity and individual
felicity ; watching with an equal and comprehensive eye over this great assemblage of
communities and interests, he laid the foundations of our national policy in the unerring,
immutable principles of morality, based on
religion, exemplifying the pre-eminence of
a free government, by all the attributes which
win the affections of its citizens, or command
the respect of the world.

    " O fortunatos nimium, sua si bona norint!"

LEADING through the complicated difficulties produced by previous obligations and
conflicting interests, seconded by succeeding
houses of congress, enlightened and patriotic,
he surmounted all original obstruction, and
brightened the path of our national felicity.

THE presidential term expiring, his solicitude to exchange exaltation for humility,
returned with a force, increased with increase of age ; and he had prepared his fare-
well address to his countrymen, proclaim-
ing his intention, when the united interposi-

tion of all around him, enforced by the
eventful prospects of the epoch, produced a
further sacrifice of inclination to duty. The
election of president followed, and WASH-
INGTON, by the unanimous vote of the nation, was called to resume the chief magistracy. What a wonderful fixture of confidence ! Which attracts most our admiration,
a people so correct, or a citizen combining
an assemblage of talents forbidding rivalry,
and stifling even envy itself ? Such a nation
ought to be happy, such a chief must be forever revered.

WAR, long menaced by the Indian tribes,
now broke out ; and the terrible conflict,
deluging Europe with blood, began to shed
its baneful influence over our happy land.
To the first, outstretching his invincible arm,
under the orders of the gallant WAYNE, the
American Eagle soared triumphant through
distant forests. Peace followed victory ; and
the melioration of the condition of the enemy, followed peace. Godlike virtue, which
uplifts even the subdued savage.

TO the second he opposed himself. New
and delicate was the conjuncture, and great
was the stake. Soon did his penetrating

mind discern and seize the only course, continuing to us all the felicity enjoyed. He issued his proclamation of neutrality. This index to his whole subsequent conduct, was sanctioned by the approbation of both houses of Congress, and by the approving voice of the people.

TO this sublime policy he inviolably adhered, unmoved by foreign intrusion, unshaken by domestic turbulence.

> " Justum et tenacem propositi virum,
> Non civium ardor prava jubentium,
> Non vultus instantis tyranni,
> Mente quatit solida."

MAINTAINING his pacific system at the expense of no duty, America, faithful to herself, and unstained in her honour, continued to enjoy the delights of peace, while afflicted Europe mourns in every quarter under the accumulated miseries of an unexampled war ; miseries in which our happy country must have shared, had not our pre-eminent WASHINGTON been as firm in council as he was brave in the field.

PURSUING stedfastly his course, he held safe the public happiness, preventing foreign war, and quelling internal discord, till the

revolving period of a third election approached, when he executed his interrupted, but in-
extinguishable desire, of returning to the
humble walks of private life.

THE promulgation of his fixed resolution,
stopped the anxious wishes of an affectionate
people, from adding a third unanimous testimonial of their unabated confidence in the
man so long enthroned in their hearts.
When before was affection like this exhibited
on earth ?—turn over the records of ancient
Greece—review the annals of mighty Rome
—examine the volumes of modern Europe ;
you search in vain. AMERICA and her
WASHINGTON only afford the dignified
exemplification.

THE illustrious personage called by the
national voice in succession to the arduous
office of guiding a free people, had new difficulties to encounter : The amicable effort of
settling our difficulties with France, begun
by WASHINGTON, and pursued by his successor in virtue as in station, proving abortive, America took measures of self-defence.
No sooner was the public mind roused by a
prospect of danger, than every eye was turn-

ed to the friend of all, though fecluded from
public view, and grey in public fervice. The
virtuous veteran, following his plough, received the unexpected fummons with mingled emotions of indignation at the unmerited
ill-treatment of his country, and of a determination once more to risk his all in her defence.

THE annunciation of these feelings, in his
affecting letter to the president, accepting
the command of the army, concludes his official conduct.

FIRST in war, first in peace, and first in
the hearts of his countrymen, he was second
to none in the humble and endearing scenes
of private life : pious, just, humane, temperate, and sincere ; uniform, dignified, and commanding, his example was as edifying to all
around him as were the effects of that example lasting.

TO his equals he was condescending ; to
his inferiors kind ; and to the dear object of
his affections exemplarily tender ; correct
throughout, vice shuddered in his presence,
and virtue always felt his fostering hand ;

the purity of his private character gave ef-
fulgence to his public virtues.

HIS last scene comported with the whole
tenor of his life : although in extreme pain,
not a sigh, not a groan escaped him ; and
with undisturbed serenity he closed his well
spent life. Such was the man America has
lost ! such was the man for whom our nation mourns !

METHINKS I see his august image, and
hear, falling from his venerable lips, these
deep sinking words :

" CEASE, SONS of AMERICA, lamenting
our separation : go on, and confirm by your
wisdom the fruits of our joint councils, joint
efforts, and common dangers. Reverence
religion ; diffuse knowledge throughout
your land ; patronize the arts and sciences ;
let liberty and order be inseparable companions ; controul party spirit, the bane of free
government ; observe good faith to, and cultivate peace with all nations ; shut up every
avenue to foreign influence ; contract rather
than extend national connexions ; rely on
yourselves only—be American in thought
and deed. Thus will you give immortality

to that union, which was the constant object
of my terrestrial labours : thus will you preserve undisturbed to the latest posterity, the
felicity of a people to me most dear ; and
thus will you supply (if my happiness is
now aught to you) the only vacancy in the
round of pure bliss high heaven bestows."

A PROCLAMATION.

BY THE *PRESIDENT* OF THE UNITED STATES
OF AMERICA.

WHEREAS the Congress of the United States have this day resolved," That it be recommended to the people of the United States to assemble on the twenty-second day of February next, in such numbers and manner as may be convenient, publicly to testify their grief for the death of Gen. GEORGE WASHINGTON, by suitable eulogies, orations and discourses, or by public prayers :" and, " That the President be requested to issue a proclamation for the purpose of carrying the foregoing resolution into effect." NOW, THEREFORE, I, JOHN ADAMS, President of the United States of America, do hereby proclaim the same accordingly.

GIVEN under my hand and the seal of the United States, at Philadelphia, the sixth day of January, in the year of our Lord, one thousand eight hundred, and of the independence of the said states the twenty fourth.

JOHN ADAMS.

By the President,
TIMOTHY PICKERING, Secretary of State.

PARTICULAR ACCOUNT
OF THE LATE ILLNESS AND DEATH OF
GEORGE WASHINGTON.

SOME time in the night of Friday, the 10th instant, having been exposed to a rain on the preceding day, General WASHINGTON was attacked with an inflammatory affection of the upper part of the wind pipe, called in technical language *Cynache Trachealis*. The disease commenced with a violent ague, accompanied with some pain in the upper and fore part of the throat, a sense of stricture in the same part, a cough, and a difficult, rather than a painful deglutition, which were soon succeeded by fever and a quick and laborious respiration. The necessity of bloodletting suggesting itself to the General, he procured a bleeder in the neighbourhood, who took from his arm in the night twelve or fourteen ounces of blood. He could not by any means be prevailed on by the family to send for the attending physician till the following morning, who arrived at Mount Vernon at about 11 o'clock on Saturday. Discovering the case to be highly alarming, and foreseeing the fatal tendency of the dis-

ease, two consulting physicians were immediately sent for, who arrived, one at half after three, and the other at four o'clock in
the afternoon : in the mean time were employed two pretty copious bleedings, a blister
was applied to the part affected, two moderate doses of calomel were given, and an in-
jection was administered, which operated on
the lower intestines, but all without any per-
ceptible advantage, the respiration becoming
still more difficult and distressing. Upon the
arrival of the first of the consulting physicians, it was agreed, as there were yet no
signs of accumulation in the bronchial ves-
sels of the lungs, to try the result of another
bleeding, when about thirty-two ounces of
blood were drawn, without the smallest apparent alleviation of the disease. Vapours of
vinegar and water were frequently inhaled,
ten grains of calomel were given, succeeded
by repeated doses of emetic tartar, amounting in all to five or six grains, with no other
effect than a copious discharge from the bow-
els. The powers of life seemed now mani-
festly yielding to the force of the disorder ;
blisters were applied to the extremities, together with a cataplasm of bran and vinegar

S

to the throat. Speaking, which was painful
from the beginning, now became almost impracticable ; respiration grew more and more
contracted and imperfect, till half after 11
on Saturday night, retaining the full possession of his intellect—when he expired without a struggle.

HE was fully impressed at the beginning
of his complaint, as well as through every
succeeding stage of it, that its conclusion
would be mortal ; submitting to the several
exertions made for his recovery, rather as a
duty, than from any expectation of their efficacy. He considered the operations of death
upon his system as cœval with the disease ;
and several hours before his death, after repeated efforts to be understood, succeeded in
expressing a desire that he might be permitted to die without further interruption.

DURING the short period of his illness, he
economized his time, in the arrangement of
such few concerns as required his attention,
with the utmost serenity ; and anticipated his
approaching dissolution with every demon-
stration of that equanimity for which his

whole life has been so uniformly and singularly conspicuous.

JAMES CRAIK, *Attending Physician.*
ELISHA C. DICK, *Consulting Physician.*

WASHINGTON's FUNERAL.

Extract of a letter from a correspondent in Alexandria, dated Dec. 19, 1799.

" YESTERDAY I attended the Funeral of the saviour of our country at Mount Vernon ; and had the honour of being one who carried his body to the vault. He was borne by military gentlemen, and brethren of our lodge, of which he was formerly master. I inclose you a sketch of the procession. To describe the scene is impossible. The coffin bore his sword and apron ; and the members of the lodge walked as mourners. His horse was led, properly caparisoned, by two of his servants, in mourning.

" AS I helped place his body in the vault, and stood at the door while funeral service was performing, I had the best opportunity of observing the countenances of all. Every

one was affected, but none so much as his
domestics of all ages."

INTERMENT.

Georgetown, December 20, 1799.

ON Wednesday last, the mortal part of
WASHINGTON the great—the father of his
country and the friend of man, was consigned
to the tomb, with solemn honours and funeral pomp.

A MULTITUDE of persons assembled, from
many miles around, at Mount Vernon, the
choice abode and last residence of the illustrious chief. There were the groves, the
spacious avenues, the beautiful and sublime
scenes, the noble mansion ; but, alas ! the
august inhabitant was now no more. That
great soul was gone. His mortal part was
there indeed ; but ah ! how affecting ! how
awful the spectacle of such worth and greatness, thus, to mortal eyes, fallen : yes ! fallen !
fallen !

IN the long and lofty portico, where oft
the hero walked in all his glory, now lay the

shrouded corpse. The countenance still composed and serene, seemed to express the dignity of the spirit which lately dwelt in that lifeless form. There those who paid the last sad honours to the benefactor of his country, took an impressive, a farewel view.

ON the ornament, at the head of the coffin, was inscribed SURGE AD JUDICIUM ; about the middle of the coffin, GLORIA DEO ; and on the silver plate,

GENERAL
George Washington,
DEPARTED THIS LIFE, ON THE 14th DEC. 1799, Æt. 68.

BETWEEN three and four o'clock, the sound of artillery from a vessel in the river, firing minute guns, awoke afresh our solemn sorrow ; the corpse was moved ; a band of music with mournful melody, melted the soul into all the tenderness of woe.

THE procession was formed and moved on in the following order :

Cavalry,
Infantry, } with arms reversed. } Guard,

Music,

Clergy,

THE general's horse, with his saddle, holsters, and pistols.

Col. SIMMS,   Col. GILPIN,

Col. RAMSAY,   Col. MARSTELLER,

Col. PAYNE,   Col. LITTLE,

Mourners,

Masonic Brethren,

Citizens.

WHEN the procession had arrived at the bottom of the elevated lawn, on the banks of the Potomac, where the family vault is placed, the cavalry halted, the infantry marched towards the Mount and formed the inlines ; the clergy, the masonic brothers, and the citizens, descended to the vault, and the funeral service of the church was performed. The firing was repeated from the vessel in the river, and the sounds echoed from the woods and hills around.

THREE general discharges by the infantry, the cavalry, and eleven pieces of artillery, which lined the banks of the Potomac
back of the vault, paid the last tribute to the
entombed commander in chief of the armies
of the United States, and to the venerable
departed hero.

THE sun was now setting. Alas! the
SUN OF GLORY was set forever. No—the
name of WASHINGTON, the American
President and General will triumph over
death; the unclouded brightness of his glory
will illuminate future ages.

PRESIDENT's MESSAGE.

MR. SHAW, secretary to the president,
communicated the following message:

Gentlemen of the Senate, and
Gentlemen of the House of Representatives,

IN compliance with the request in one
of the resolutions of Congress of the 21st of
December last, I transmitted a copy of those
resolutions by my secretary, Mr. SHAW, to
Mrs. WASHINGTON, assuring her of the profound respect Congress will ever bear to her

person and character ; of their condolence in
the late afflicting dispensation of providence,
and intreating her assent to the interment of
the remains of General GEORGE WASH-
INGTON, in the manner expressed in the
first resolution. As the sentiments of that
virtuous lady, not less beloved by this nation
than she is at present greatly afflicted, can
never be so well expressed as in her own
words ; I transmit to Congress her original
letter.

IT would be an attempt of too much delicacy, to make any comments upon it ; but
there can be no doubt, that the nation at
large, as well as all the branches of the government, will be highly gratified by any arrangement which may diminish the sacrifice
she makes of her individual feelings.

JOHN ADAMS.

United States, Jan. 8, 1800.

M*RS*. WASHINGTON's LETTER.

Mount Vernon, Dec. 31, 1799.

SIR,

WHILE I feel with keenest anguish, the
late dispensation of Divine Providence, I

cannot be insensible to the mournful tributes of respect and veneration, which are paid to the memory of my dear deceased husband ; and, as his best services and most anxious wishes, were always devoted to the welfare and happiness of his country, to know that they were truly appreciated, and gratefully remembered, affords no inconsiderable consolation.

TAUGHT by the great example, which I have so long had before me, never to oppose my private wishes to the public will, I must consent to the request made by congress, which you have had the goodness to transmit me, and in doing this, I need not, I cannot say, what a sacrifice of individual feeling I make to a sense of public duty.

WITH grateful acknowledgment and unfeigned thanks for the personal respect, and evidences of condolence, expressed by Congress and yourself, I remain very respectfully, sir, your most obedient and humble servant,

MARTHA WASHINGTON.

The President of the United States.

T

BIOGRAPHICAL OUTLINE

OF

General George Washington,

BY J. M. WILLIAMS.

WHEN a man of so much importance, and an object of such general estimation, as the illustrious character under consideration, is removed from the busy theatre of life, a more than ordinary curiosity is excited, to know in what manner he exercised his being, and by what degrees he rose to an elevation so renowned and so glorious.

THE late GENERAL GEORGE WASHINGTON, was born in Virginia, in the parish of Washington, in Westmoreland county, on the 22d day of February, 1732 : his father, Mr. *Augustine Washington*, was the owner of an ample estate, comprehending a large plantation and a farm, in Virginia, and a gentleman of enviable endowments and much respectability. The ancestors of this valued man arrived in that part of America, from the county of York, in Great-Britain, in the year 1657, and established a settlement in King George's county. During the first movement of the revolutionary war, the late General WASHINGTON had three brothers and one sister living, viz. *Samuel, John,* and *Charles,* each of whom had estates of consequence—the lady was married to Colonel *Fielding Lewis.*

THE general's father married twice, and our political saviour was the first issue of the second marriage ; his education was conducted under the superintendence of his father, who had his boy trained up in those exercises and feats of activity and hardihood, as steeled his young nerves and fitted him for the purposes of an enterprising life : by this judicious proceeding, he was rendered muscular and healthful, and, as the mind is greatly dependent on the body, his intellect became sound, and his apprehension lively. His hours of study were guided by a private tutor, who infused that correct taste for composition, which he has so charmingly exemplified in his correspondence and official papers ; and those sentiments of morality,which

made his philosophy amiable and his practice noble.

THE prominent course of his tuition involved the theory of the Latin language, the
problems of Euclid, and the prosody of his
vernacular tongue. His father died when
he was a boy, and he fell under the guardian-
ship of his elder brother, Mr. *Lawrence Washington.*—When admiral *Vernon* was employed in the reduction of Carthagena, this gentleman accompanied the expedition, and had
the command of a company in the colonial
troops; at the termination of that exploit,
he returned and married the daughter of the
Hon. *William Fairfax*, of Bellevoir. He took
his lady to the family seat, which he civilly
denominated *Mount Vernon*, in remembrance
and in honour of the gallant admiral, who
had expressed a predilection for the talents
and spirit of the young American. This
gentleman was created adjutant general of
the Virginia militia, and died soon after the
appointment. The daughter of this gentleman, and his second brother, being deceased,
General WASHINGTON succeeded to the family patrimony, and sat down as the legiti-
mate lord of an extensive and rich do-
main.

WHEN no more than fifteen years of age, he was enrolled as a midshipman in the British service, but his destiny had ordered it otherwise; his mother entered her protest against the proceeding, and the idea was abandoned.

BEFORE he was a complete adult, and while under twenty, he obtained the rank of major in a Virginian battalion, the original office of adjutant general, as filled by his deceased brother, being trisected in authority and given to three several districts, as the province had increased in population equal to a justification of the division.

SHORTLY after this military induction, an event happened, which, in its progress, called into action those eminent powers for negotiation and politic address, which have been so conspicuously exerted since, in the defence of his country's immunities, and the arrangement of her full and equal laws.

IN 1753 the French, from the Canadas, suborned some Indian tribes to assist them in plundering the western frontiers, in the neighbourhood of the Alleghany and Ohio rivers. The imperial country hearing of the

aggression, instructed the governor and council of the Virginia province to repel the in-
vasion by force : they, notwithstanding, believed it as the more prudent step to attempt
an explanation with the French and Indians,
and thereby prevent the effusion of human
blood. It was resolved, on mature deliberation, to depute Major WASHINGTON on this
arduous and critical embassy. He conveyed
a letter to the commander in chief of the enemy's forces, explanatory of the violation,
and made some friendly overtures to the
six nations and their allies, to induce them
to become attached to the British interest :
he began his journey in the earlier part of
the winter, accompanied by a few persons,
and after traversing immense forests and
pathless deserts, he happily arrived at the
quarters of Monsieur *de St. Pierre*, to whom
he communicated the nature and letter of
his mission, and the interview was conducted on his part with so much precaution,
temper, and firmness, that it was ultimately
successful. His management of the Indians
was not less propitious.—For this momentous service, he received the warm approval of
lieutenant governor *Dinwiddie* in particular,

and his country in general. He kept a diary or journal during this novel progress, which has been since published to the world, and proved entertaining and instructive, but more especially to those who have travelled into those remote parts of the continent. It was in this publication that he first manifested that love of method, force of reasoning, and constancy to a resolution comprehensively founded, which have since so characterised him in arranging the elements of order, and establishing the liberties of his nation.

ALTHOUGH Major WASHINGTON had perfected the object of his embassy, so far as a written stipulation could bind, it was soon discovered that the enemy was not faithful to his word and bond of honour, as the warlike movements on the western frontier plainly evinced. In this distressing time, an order arrived from Britain to embody the troops of the colonies for their common defence : the state of Virginia was the first in obedience to this command, and in the year 1754, raised an appropriate sum of money and a regiment of 400 men, to assemble on the frontiers of their colony. Mr. *Fry*, a pro-

fessor in the College of William and Mary,
had the command of this corps, and Major
WASHINGTON, at the age of twenty three,
was nominated Lieutenant Colonel. The
commander dying before the regiment was
perfected, his rank and power devolved on
the subject of this memoir.

COLONEL WASHINGTON thus invested, re-
doubled his diligence in exercising his men,
fixing magazines, and opening roads : it was
his hope to have established a military post
at the junction of the Alleghany and Monongahela rivers, a measure of precaution
which he had warmly recommended to the
council the preceding year. To this important spot (now called Pittsburg) he directed
his march in May, without waiting for rein-
forcements, either regular or provincial, so
great was his eagerness to fortify that station.

IN his progress he encountered a considerable party of French and Indians, at a place
called Redstone : he instantly charged and
routed them, making prisoners and destroying fifty, among the captives was Monsieur
De La Force, and two other officers. Colonel
WASHINGTON then understood the perils of

his situation, as these gentlemen informed him that the French had 1000 regular troops on the Ohio and a numerous party of savages ; and what was more immediately distressing, that they had pre-occupied the post at the confluence of the rivers, and had named it fort *Du Quesne.*

IN this dilemma, he took his stand at a spot called Great Meadows, to procure forage, and erected a stockade for his stores, which he called *Fort Necessity.* He waited the arrival of succours from the neighbouring colonies, but was only strengthened by Captain *Mackay's* regulars, which made his force, in the aggregate, but 400 efficient men. The enemy lay dormant until July, when he understood that a strong reconnoitring party was approaching rapidly : he was prompt in his decision on the aspect of danger ; he sallied out with his little army and defeated his foe ; but this vigorous effort for his security was ineffectual, as shortly after, a large detachment of French and Indians, to the amount of 1500 men, under the command of the *Sieur de Villiers,* attacked him in his temporary fortification—the assailed made a firm resistance, and killed 200 of the enemy, but lost, in killed or wounded, many of their gallant comrades. This determined opposition so discomfited the French leader, that a parley was offered on his part and accepted, and an honourable capitulation was the consequence. The diminutive garrison marched out, with the honours of war, and their commander at their head, with baggage and military stores: the provincial soldiers were plundered and massacreed, during their retreat, by the savages; after this discomfiture, the skeleton of the Virginian regiment returned to Alexandria, to re-fill their ranks and repose after their disasters.

WHEN the British ambassador remonstrated at the court of Versailles, on the infraction of the articles of capitulation, it was perceived that the French officers in America had acted agreeable to their instructions; the real views of the christian king, in respect to the colonies in America, then under British subjugation, were now developed; and after this disclosure, the French became more active in their hostile preparations, which were pursued without remission through the winter of 1754, and the spring of 1755.

THE government of Virginia did not remain regardless of the machinations and aggressions of the French. They erected forts Cumberland and Loudon, and ordered a camp at Wills Creek, from which situation they could harrass their enemies on the Ohio. In the furtherance of these designs, Colonel WASHINGTON was highly useful, and his services were acknowledged in terms of respect and approval.

IT was at this period when the ill-fated General *Braddock* arrived in America from Britain : he landed at Alexandria, with two old regiments from Ireland, and to these were to be united the different corps in America, including the independent and provincial bodies ; at the head of this combined force he was to crush the bold and cruel invaders of our frontiers. On this occasion the the evils of etiquette were permitted to annull the recommendations of virtue ; a royal definition of rank had prevailed, which ridiculously signified, that no officer who had not derived his commission *immediately* from his majesty, could command one who had been blessed with that honour. When this distinction was understood, Colonel WASH-

INGTON resigned his commission, but he did not suffer his disgust, arising from the forms and fopperies of a court, to supercede the regards he bore towards his country : he entered the army as a volunteer, and condescended to serve as an extra aid de camp to General *Braddock*. The army marched by Wills Creek for fort Du Quesne, and in this route Colonel WASHINGTON's counsel would have proved the salvation of the army, had it been duly taken and followed ; as no person, in the colony, was so thoroughly acquainted with the advantages and disadvantages connected with the various stations in this march, as himself ; but on this event, as in others, the presumption of arrogance involved the destruction of its own agency. General *Braddock* disdained to be instructed by a provincial officer, and he perished in his folly : in the course of the march he met, unexpectedly and without adequate preparation, a large body of the foe, when a bloody conflict instantly ensued, which ended in the defeat of *Braddock's* army, which consisted of 2000 regulars and 800 provincials : the slaughter of the British troops was great, and their extermination would have occurred, had not the intrepid and discreet WASH-

INGTON, aided by his colonial adherents, covered their retreat, which they effected in the utmost confusion and dismay ; when Col. WASHINGTON had conducted them safely over the ford of the Monongahela, and the enemy ceasing to pursue their career, he thought it expedient to consult with Col. *Dunbar*, who was left in the rear with the second division of the army and the baggage : in pursuance of this idea, he was constrained to travel all night, on horseback, through a gloomy and untrodden forest, and was so exhausted on his arrival, by such a variety of fatigue, that he was supported by pillows. It may not be unnecessary to remark that he was the only officer, who was mounted during the battle, that was not killed or wounded. The European accounts of this memorable and calamitous affair, were not unmixed with abundant praises on his skill, his perseverance and gallantry.

SHORTLY after this overthrow, the arrangement of rank, so injuriously unpleasant to the colonial officers, was altered, and the government of Virginia, bestowed on Colonel WASHINGTON, the command of all the troops raised, and to be raised, in the colony :

he maintained this commission with honour, until 1759, when the restoration of tranquility on the frontiers took place, and he resigned his command : he was additionally induced to this resignation, by the personal inconveniences of a pulmonary disease, the probable enfeebling effect of a life of thought, hazard, toil and inconvenience. The officers and private soldiers, which formed the Virginia line, would not permit their beloved commander to retire without following him to his retreat, with an unanimous testimonial of their veneration of his character, and their regret at his resolution : he received this token of their unaffected regard, with manly tenderness, and even increased their love towards him, by proving himself so uniformly worthy of its fulness.

HE had not receded long from the bustle and horrors of a campaign, and the customs of a soldier's duty, before his health was happily increased : it was at this epoch that he married Mrs. *Martha Custis*, a young and beautiful widow, " with whom he had a fortune of twenty thousand pounds sterling in her own right, besides her dower in one of the principal estates in Virginia ;"

on the consummation of this union, Colonel
WASHINGTON and his lady, equal in years,
suavity, and virtue, settled at Mount Vernon.

IN this scene of domestic felicity, he commenced planter and farmer, and managed
his agricultural concerns so discreetly and
prosperously, that he has been held forth as
an example deserving universal imitation.—
Colonel WASHINGTON was one of the greatest landholders in North America : his estate
at Mount Vernon was computed, in 1787,
to consist of nine thousand acres, under his
own management and cultivation ; he had
likewise various large tracts of land in other
parts of the state ; his annual receipt from
his estates, amounted, in 1776, to *four thous-
and pounds sterling*, and it was then believed
would have sold for upwards of *one hundred
and sixty thousand pounds sterling*, which is
equal to more than 666,000 dollars. What
his revenue was recently we do not know,
but their can be little presumption in suppos-
ing that it was much increased, under his
prudential guidance and practical economy.

HE allotted a part of the Saturday, in each week, to receive the reports of his overseers, which were registered progressively, to enable him to compare the labour with the produce of each particular part ; and, it is affirmed, that this weekly retrospect, was duly considered by this great man, during the stormy movements of the revolutionary war, and his presidency of the United States.—He has raised, in one year, seven thousand bushels of wheat, and ten thousand bushels of Indian corn, on his Mount Vernon estate : in a succeeding year he raised two hundred lambs, sowed twenty seven bushels of flax-seed, and planted seven hundred bushels of potatoes ; at the same time his domestics manufactured linen and woollen cloth enough for his numerous household, which amounted to nearly a thousand persons : with him, regularity and industry was the order of each day, and the consequent reflection made them all happy.

THOUGH agriculture was pursued by him with such undeviating attention, he used it rather as the means of his pleasure than the end of his wishes ; which concentrated in the labour to improve the well being of his fellow citizens, and to effect this he desisted from planting tobacco, to employ himself in the introduction and fostering such articles of vegetation, as might ultimately tend to a national advantage.—The first passion of his heart was the love of his country, and the tone of that high and inspiriting impulse was never broken : it was equally visible and predominant in the senate end the field ; it was mingled in the energies of his occupation, and it pervaded the vision in his dream.

THE excellence and usefulness of General WASHINGTON, was always apparent, and his seeming more brilliant and dignified at one period than another, did not arise from any alteration of his principle, but the splendour of the service. From the year 1759, to the year 1774, he was a member of assembly, a magistrate of the county in which he resided, and a judge of the court, and in each capacity he was as able, as assiduous, and as incorrupt, as in any of his more exalted offices. He was elected a delegate to the first congress in 1774, and to that which associated in the ensuing year.

W

ON the 15th of June, 1775, he had the supreme honour to be unanimously appointed, by this immortal assembly of sages and patriots, commander in chief of all the forces raised, or to be raised, for the resistance of oppression and the maintenance of their colonial privileges. He accepted the appointment with gratitude and apprehension ; the manner with which he tinctured his zeal for the public good, with doubts of his own personal sufficiency, was illustrative of human greatness : the disinterested tenor of his reply to the president on his nomination, was equally endearing as his modesty, and should be held in eternal admiration.

IT was a circumstance very fortunate for the existence of human liberty, that this nomination, by the council of the states, should be unattended with the customary emotions of personal envy, and commonly approved by the people : he had become proverbial for his honour, moderation and bravery,and was conspicuous for his caution : and with these powerful recommendations in his behalf, he was not only invested with confidence,but followed with joy.

GENERAL WASHINGTON arrived at the camp at Cambridge, on July 2d, 1776, and took the command of the American army : he was saluted on his arrival with every mark of satisfaction ; the troops expressed their exultation on beholding their leader, who began the necessary work of organization and discipline ; without which, an army degenerates into a mob, and is rather an incumbrance than a bulwark.

IT is not precisely within our province, nor is it in our capability to pursue him through the mazes of the different actions in which he was engaged, nor to detail those " hair breadth 'scapes" with which his progress was chequered ; there were times when the destruction of his band of heroes seemed inevitable, and the most sanguine lover of his country began to despond—but the singular penetration of General WASHINGTON enabled him to elude the imminent dangers, and disconcert the operations of the ablest generals of Britain : yet, notwithstanding these instances of preservation, he felt much uneasiness and mortification from the smallness of his force, contending against a host of veterans, perfect in dis-

cipline and high in spirit. Perhaps few
troops have contended with a longer series
of disasters, than those disciples of liberty,
in their struggle to uphold the primary immunities of man.

TWO base and treacherous attempts were
discovered, about this time ; one was directed against the life of General WASHINGTON,
and the other against his reputation : Governor *Tryon* had suborned the then mayor of
Newyork, to assist the royal forces on their
arrival in that city, and General WASHING-
TON was to be assassinated : this detestable
design was rendered abortive by apprehend-
ing *Thomas Hickey*, one of General WASHING-
TON's life-guard men, who was engaged in
the conspiracy, and had engaged others ; this
false miscreant was tried by a court martial
on the 28th of June, found guilty, and was
executed at eleven o'clock the same day,
amidst the curses of the American army.
The other malignant proceeding originated
with an officer of high rank, who was so
mean as to envy the superiority of another,
and so vindictive as to circulate calumny for
his overthrow : but this endeavour was
soon frustrated, and the author became con-

temptible : it should be noted that this was the only occasion, on which the ability and integrity of General WASHINGTON was ever questioned, but it proved as weak in its consequences, as it was wicked in contemplation.

FROM the first action which he commanded in this dreadful contest, when he compelled the British troops to evacuate Boston, by a victory unstained with blood, to the august termination of the struggle in 1781, he was always the same philosophic hero; he was an uncommon man, fitted for uncommon difficulties, and, happily for the interests of the new world, it was so ordered by providence, that his mighty trials, were but " squared to his proportionate strength," his intelligence corresponded with his intrepidity, and he was graced with both *Minervas* : the alacrity of his mind felt no decay from disappointment : the resources of his capacity were commensurate to the perils as they arose : he regarded the caprices of fortune with steadiness, and knowing that his cause was just, he relied, with firmness, on his dauntless followers and the will of heaven.

IN 1783 a general peace was negotiated
and concluded in Europe, and then the proud
hour arrived, when this great man had finished all the labours of his military life ; he
entered Newyork in triumph, amidst the ac-
clamations of a liberated people : he was not
decorated with the *fasces* or *insignia* of a Ro-
man warrior, nor did he drag the representatives of a plundered province at his chariot
wheels, in bondage and in chains : his dignity and solacement were derived from a purer
source ; he brought the assurance of manu-
mission to a suffering world, and bade them
prepare a charter for the security of their
rescued privileges.

HE resigned his commission, as commander in chief, to Congress, which he had used
with such wonderful advantage to his country, but without ostentation or any accom-
panyment of vanity ; and returned, with
gladness, to the bosom of his family at
Mount Vernon. As he passed through the
intermediate towns and villages, all ages and
degrees poured forth, to welcome, with the
tenderest congratulations, the deliverer of
his country : they offered up their artless
supplications, to the throne of mercy, to bless

and preserve their common benefactor, and those unadulterated tokens of regard must have made a deep and felicitous impression on a heart such as he possessed.

REPEATED offers of compensation were now made him, by the various states, for his manifold services, but he declined them all, and even those which might only liquidate the additional expences he had incurred in the public cause : his enlarged mind felt superior to such considerations, he was satisfied with having run a race of glory, and drew his richest rewards from his own sensations : his desires were bounded by honour ; he had all the self denial and magnanimity so attributable to *Scipio,* but the point of his heroism had a more philanthropic direction.

FROM the peace of 1783 to 1787, he passed his time in a rotation of civil and social duties, arranging and methodizing his domestic concerns ; maintaining an extensive correspondence with eminent personages at home and abroad ; perusing works of science ; examining experiments in arts, and the amazing phenomena of nature, and receiv-

ing the visits and homage of illustrious for-
eigners and natives, who were incessantly
crouding to Mount Vernon, to salute its be-
nignant owner.

IN 1787 he was called to a seat in that
convention, which sat in Philadelphia, to
assist in the stupendous and difficult task of
making a new constitution for the United
States; and of that venerable assemblage,
that constellation of sages, he was chosen
president : when the several articles of this
inestimable obligation were digested and ma-
tured, it was issued for the observance of his
happy countrymen, and the admiration of
the universe : its provisions had been duly
weighed and ameliorated, by his inquisitive
and comprehensive understanding, and it received a prompt currency under the influence of his name.

IT is a simple, beautiful structure, made
up with skill from liberal grants and concessions, and as perfect in its component
parts as such an instrument of legation can
be, which professes to combine social security with individual liberty : we do not insist
so unequivocally upon the strength of this

compact, as that is materially dependent upon the wisdom and morality of those it is
calculated to govern : man, as a species, is
more liable to the impressions of delusion
than of truth; and, notwithstanding he is rational, must be guarded and limited in his
agency, lest the indulgence of his own inor-
dinate desires, should de detrimental to the
happiness of all.

WERE it possible to persuade mankind,
what is their chief interest here to know,
that to assist the good endeavours, and to
sympathize with the weaknesses and necessi-
ties of each other, yields an enjoyment far
superior to any of a mere selfish nature ; there
would be little occasion, in a moral view, to
threaten the infliction either of temporal or
eternal punishment.   Indeed it seems almost
sufficiently just, if there be any totally desti-
tute of humanity, that such, from their dul-
ness or malignity, are deprived of the most
exquisite and exalted felicity.

ON the 30th of April, 1789, he was invested as president of the United States, in
Newyork, and his investiture was hailed and
accompanied by the unfeigned rapture of his

fellow citizens. He then entered upon one
of the most solemn offices that man can possibly assume : to administer a government of
novel elements : to organize the high republican departments of state, and give to each
its due nerve, ramification, and civic depen-
dencies : to make the effect as parallel as
possible with popular expectation, yet to
ward against any irrational infringement so
far, as that the whole might be ultimately
practicable and durable : but the national
confidence attended his exertions, and that
confidence was well reposed, as he began his
supreme delegation with principles of virtue.
The pleasures of virtue, are, first, the immediate satisfaction we enjoy in contributing to
the advantage of others, virtue in this case
being its own best reward ; not that it bestows because it receives, but that it receives
because it is disposed to bestow, as a lumin-
ous body is yet more enlightened by the reflection of its own splendour.

To declare that he administered the obligations of his great office with propriety,
would be but a feeble acknowledgment : he
stepped forward with modest hesitation,
in obedience to the public voice, to give or-

der, and harmony, and force, to the chaotic
and untried principles of a new scheme of
rule, and he accomplished all that a human
being could ; he defined the extent of the
common charter of his nation ; and, in the
hazardous performance of the contract, he
laid the foundation of such a pure and liberal
system of ethical policy, as no confederation
of people had heretofore known ; he knew
what portion of liberty perturbed man could
bear, and he was solicitous that he should
have as much as he was fitted to enjoy.

IN the decline of the same year, in which
he had consented to bear the incumbent
weight of the young republic, he visited the
eastern states, and was saluted by all classes
of the inhabitants, with fervor, love, and duty. The congratulations he experienced,
were such as monarchs might envy : the respect he met was of that unsophisticated nature, in which the soul makes its offering
with the body—every municipal and religious community addressed him on his arrival; and, in his answers to these affectionate
memorials of public esteem, he had the wisdom to disseminate such documents, as
might operate to an obedience of the laws,

and to uphold morality ; knowing, that we
can have no practice of goodness, or calmness of mind, but what is connected with
moral beauty.

WHEN the presidential term had expired,
he indicated a resolution to return once
more to the shades of domestic retirement,
as the infirmities of age had rendered him
less vigorous ; he had even pondered upon
his farewel address, and was preparing for a
final secession from the affairs of state, when
his apprehensive countrymen, united to implore him to desist from such an abandon-
ment of office : their interposition super-
ceded his own will, and he was inducted
in the chief magistracy, a second time, to the
manifest satisfaction of all honest men in
America !

THE good sense and probity of a people,
was never more conspicuous, than in this
cautious proceeding ; as it is not altogether
problematical, but the very existence of the
commonwealth depended upon this timely
adoption : the moral and political world
were then trembling with the effect of a con-
vulsion, which threatened, in its progress,

to overthrow the institutes of subordination, and rebarbarize mankind : and the imposing speciousness of the innovation constituted its evil—an extraordinary and vast revolution took place in France, at once delighting, amazing, and affrighting the universe : this was an event of such portentous magnitude and dreadful splendour, as made the members of the old establishments shudder, lest the finger of reform should expose their hideousness, and crumble the feudal fabrics of antiquity into dust ; as they had become too rotten to be touched, even by the talisman of virtue. They saw the regal diadem abused, and the monastic authorities totter ; the monk and the courtier cashiered, and all the gothic privileges of pride vanish and dissolve in air : the patrician began to doubt his preeminence, and slavery hurled the chain at his oppressor : a new code of slip-shod morals was obtruded upon credulity, and the young calendar of the hour took the vizor from the seasons : the solemnity of the altar was invaded by a civic dance, and the laws of matrimony were obliterated by the voluptuaries of *Epicurus* : they encumbered a figure with tawdry habiliments that they called *reason*, and made her violate the

law and the prophets : this limitless en-
franchisement of the passions, made the
thoughtless frantic, and the thinking weep :
as the causes which produced this issue were
lost in time, so the consequences of its influence were beyond the reach of calculation : when the first sensations of monarch-
ical consternation had subsided, an expanded
and decided system of counteraction was
put in force, and a war commenced, with a
peculiar feature of horror ; not for the recovery of a province, or to assert the dignity of an insulted empire, but for the overthrow of prejudice and the extermination of
principle.

THE progress of these commotions, had
an obvious tendency to agitate the people of
the united States, many of whom were
transported with zeal, at the supposed liber-
ation of so many millions of their fellow
creatures : liberty feasts were held in the
large towns, and such inflammatory measures
pursued as were inconsistent with the pacific
views of the government : many insiduous
arts were used to involve the country in a
war with GreatBritain ; and the French faction, directing the current of the lunacy,

were incessant in their intrigues, when General WASHINGTON published his declaration of neutrality, and saved the nation.

THIS act of salvation was the result of mature thought ; the crisis, in which he resolved on the proclamation, was pregnant with infinite calamity ; he risked the durability of his hard and well earned reputation, by thus firmly opposing the indiscreet spirit of the time, but he saw the direct relation of the folly, and its ultimate mischief : both houses of Congress ratified the deed, and he pursued his exalted functions with stability, circumspection, delicacy, and honour. His conduct, during this perilous conjuncture, was, perhaps, the greatest proof of his sagacity and magnanimity, that occurred in the history of his brilliant life : the love he bore his country subdued all minor considerations ; he had the greatness to be just and kind towards those, who seemed eager to be destroyed in the gratification of an indigested desire : by this determined step he paralized the arm of sedition, but it had the unavoidable effect of partially jarring the chords of public harmony : yet the bond of amity between the president and the people was

unsullied : the inquietude was diminished,
in proportion as the measure was understood, and although dissension ever did, and
ever will, happen in the best regulated governments, the prevailing part of a nation constantly veer towards the points of reciprocal justice.

As the discontents, arising from this great
effort of policy, have not wholly subsided,
it may not be improper to suppose
the motives which actuated the supreme
magistrate : he saw that the conservation of
the civil order was endangered by this illegit-
imate novelty, which undermined the base
of mutual protection and personal comfort ;
he knew that the national character of his
countrymen was forming, and he was unwilling that any of their habitudes should
be derived from Gallic deformity : he gath-
ered but little felicity from the *Decades*
and misbegotten mummeries of the French
Directory, being assured that they were in-
roads incompatible with the dignity and permanent good of human nature : their aboli-
tion of the sabbath, with its annexed piety
and consolation, and corrective ordinances,
was not, with him, an event of consummate

glory : he believed and felt that an observance of its balmy duties allured us to resignation in the sweetest way, and that our delights were even unauthorized without gratitude—to those dark spirits, whose faith is
bounded by their senses, we shall commit
the illustration of the advantages of an eternal oblivion.

THE embarrassments arising from this
evil, were not all the inconveniences he had
to contend with, at this era ; an Indian war
broke forth, which, in its first effects, caused
some consternation, but, by the adroitness,
skill, and intrepidity of General *Wayne*, soon
terminated in favour of his arms : a ratification of peace was then concluded between the
United States and the savages, and the president, in his comprehensive administration,
had the beneficence to make the comfort of
a prostrate foe, a leading consideration.

IN the month of September, 1796, the
time had revolved when a new election was
to occur, of an appropriate person to fill the
presidential seat : and while the public hope
was indulged, that General WASHINGTON
would accept it, for a third time ; he signi-

fied his unalterable resolution of receding from the toils of state, in an affectionate and wise ADDRESS to the nation; the letter and spirit of which, we fervently pray, may be understood and practised, from this period, to ages yet unborn.

HE resigned the mantle of authority with confidence to his successor, after dedicating *forty-five years* of his resplendent life, to the advantage of his country : it cannot surprise, that his renunciation of power should create dejection in his fellow citizens, whose impulse to action was virtue, and whose pursuit was justice : he consented to assume power for the benefit of mankind, and not for his own gratification : power is no estimable quality by itself ; it is the power of doing good alone, that is desirable to the wise.

HIS conduct, in his executive capacity, was dignified, yet condescending ;* and mer-

* ON General WASHINGTON's birth day, which was a few days ago, the city of Philadelphia was unusually gay ; every person of consequence in it, Quakers alone excepted, made it a point to visit the General on this day. As early as eleven o'clock in the morning he was prepared to receive them, and the audience lasted till three in the afternoon. The society of the Cincinnati,

ciful, yet resolute : he felt for the infirmities of humanity, and took an especial precaution, that while he guarded against the
establishment or continuance of an evil, to
make adequate allowance for the weaknesses
of our nature : he knew that the benign pur-

the clergy, the officers of the militia, and several others, who
formed a distinct body of citizens, came by themselves separately.
The foreign ministers attended in their richest dresses and most
splendid equipages.   Two large parlours were open for the reception of the gentlemen, the windows of one of which towards the
street were crowded with spectators on the outside.   The side-
board was furnished with cake and wines, whereof the visitors
partook.   I never observed so much cheerfulness before in the
countenance of General Washington ;   but it was impossible for
him to remain insensible to the attention and the compliments
paid to him on this occasion.

THE ladies of the city, equally attentive, paid their respects
to Mrs. Washington, who received them in the drawing room up
stairs.   After having visited the General most of the gentlemen
also waited upon her.   A public ball and supper terminated the
rejoicings of the day.   Not one town of any importance was there
in the whole union, where some meeting did not take place in
honour of this day.

GENERAL Washington gives no public dinners or other entertainments, except to those who are in diplomatic capacities, and
to a few families on terms of intimacy with Mrs. Washington.
Strangers, with whom he wishes to have some conversation about
agriculture or any such subject are sometimes invited to tea.
This, by many, is attributed to his saving disposition ; but it is
more just to ascribe it to his prudence and foresight   for as the
salary of the president is very small, and totally inadequate by
itself to support an expensive style of life, were he to give numerous and splendid entertainments, the same might possibly be expected from subsequent presidents, who, if their private fortunes
were not considerable, would be unable to live in the same style,
and might be exposed to many ill-natured observations, from the
relinquishment of what the people had been accustomed to; it is
most likely also that General Washington has been actuated by
these motives, because in his private capacity at Mount Vernon
every stranger meets with a hospitable reception from him.

WELDS' *Travels*

poses of every punishment of civil institution, should be rendered as obvious as possible, lest cruelty be inculcated by example.

FROM March, 1797, to July, 1798, he re-
mained tranquilly embosomed at Mount Vernon, in the performance of the amiable but
restricted duties of private life ; personify-
ing, in his own character, what that citizen
ought to be, who had the happy destination
of living under the most free and cle ment
government on earth : while he was thus
peacefully and radiantly declining to the
tomb, he was again supplicated to assist his
country ; she had been insulted and aggriev-
ed : he felt implicatcd, as an American, in
the national honour, and accepted the condition of the prayer.—The manifestation of
this patriotic acceptance, was the last official
action of this venerable man.

ON the 14th of December, 1799, he departed from this life, at his seat, at Mount
Vernon, in the sixty-eighth year of his age ;
after having reaped an harvest of glory,
commensurate with all that can be effected
by mortal greatness.

HE was as much a proficient in the arts of persuasion as any, for his influence on his countrymen was unlimited; and this influence was among the greatest triumphs of virtue. The institutions of *Quinctilian*, or the orations of *Thucydides* or *Sallust*, exhibit no rule of eloquence more charming, or more perfect than what he providentially exemplified, when he exhorted a part of the continental army, on the 15th of March, 1783, to resist the diabolical exertions of some seditious emissaries, who were labouring to estrange them from the common good : no system of science could have furnished an appeal more effectual, nor could any man have so restrained the passions of an armed multitude, but him, whose wisdom, bravery, and integrity were concomitant with each other.

THE disinterestedness of his mind was as alluring as it was noble,* and he used every

---

Item. Whereas by a law of the Commonwealth of Virginia, enacted in the year 1785, the legislature thereof was pleased (as an evidence of its approbation of the services I had rendered the public, during the Revolution, and partly, I believe, in confideration of my having suggested the vast advantages which the community would derive from the extension of its inland navigation under legislative patronage) to present me with one hundred shares, of one hundred dollars each, in the incorporated company, estab-

opportunity to promote the establishments for learning : he acted from high and be-nevolent motives, and he required no dear-er recompence than what his feelings could

lished for the purpose of extending the navigation of James River, from tide water to the mountains ;—and also with fifty shares of one hundred pounds sterling each, in the corporation of another company likewise established for the similar purpose of opening the navigation of the river Potomack, from tide water to Fort Cumberland ; the acceptance of which, although the offer was highly honorable and grateful to my feelings, was refused, as in-consistent with a principle which I had adopted, and had never departed from – viz —not to receive pecuniary compensation for any services I could render my country in its arduous struggle with Great Britain for its rights ; and because I had evaded similar propositions from other states in the union. Adding to this refu-sal, however, an intimation that, if it should be the pleasure of the legislature to permit me to appropriate the said shares to *public uses*, I would receive them on those terms with due sensibility ; and this it having consented to, in flat.ering terms, as will appear by a subsequent law and sundry resolutions, in the most ample and honorable manner—I proceed after this recital, for the more correct understanding of the case, to declare—that as it has al-ways been a source of serious regret with me, to see the youth of these United States sent to foreign countries for the purpose of education, often before their minds were formed, or they had im-bibed any adequate ideas of the happiness of their own ; contract-ing too frequently, not only habits of dissipation and extravagance, but principles unfriendly to republican government, and to the true and genuine liberties of mankind ; which, thereafter are rarely overcome.—For these reasons, it has been my ardent wish, to see a plan devised on a liberal scale, which would have a ten-dency to spread systematic ideas through all parts of this rising empire, thereby to do away local attachments and state prejudi-ces, as far as the nature of things would, or indeed ought to ad-mit, from our national councils.—Looking anxiously forward to the accomplishment of so desirable an object as this is, (in my estimation) my mind has not been able to contemplate any plan more likely to effect the measure, than the establishment of a U-NIVERSITY in a central part of the United States, to which the youths of fortune and talents, from all parts thereof, might be sent for the completion of their education in all the branches of polite literature ; in arts and sciences, in acquiring knowledge in the

afford ; yet what can be more pleasing than
self-applause, when it is confirmed by the
approbation of the good ? the ambitious
place their chief happiness in fame, the ava-
ricious in fortune, equally blind to the blessings that should follow.   To employ every
gentle method, therefore, to extend the principle of human sympathy : to improve our
finer feelings, and give to the soul a more

principles of politics and good government, and (as a matter of
infinite importance in my judgment) by associating with each o-
ther, and forming riendships in juvenile years, be enabled to free
themselves, in a proper degree from those local prejudices and
habitual jealousies, which have juft been mentioned ; and which,
when carried to excess, are never-failing sources of disquietude to
the public mind, and pregnant of mischievous consequences to
this country ; under these impressions, so fully dilated.

Item. I give and bequeath in perpetuity the fifty shares which
I hold in the Potomack company (under the aforesaid acts of the
legislature of Virginia) towards the endowment of a UNIVERSI-
TY, to be established within the limits of the district of Columbia, under the auspices of the general government, if that government should incline to extend a fostering hand towards it ; and
until such seminary is established, and the funds arising on these
shares shall be required for its support, my further WILL and DE-
SIRE is, that the profit accruing therefrom shall, whenever the dividends are made, be laid out in purchasing stock in the bank of
Columbia, or some other bank, at the discretion of my executors,
or by the Treasurer of the United States for the time being, under
the direction of Congress—provided that honorable body should
patronize the measure ; and the dividends proceeding from the
purchase of such stock, is to be vested in more stock, and so on,
until a sum, adequate to the accomplishment of the object, is obtained ; of which I have not the smallest doubt, before many
years pass away, even if no aid or encouragement is given by the
legislative authority, or from any other source.

Item. The hundred shares which I hold in the James River
company, I have given, and now confirm in perpetuity, to and
for the use and benefit o liberty hall academy, in the county of
Rockbridge, in the commonwealth of Virginia.

(Extracts from *WASHINGTON's* Will.)

tender touch of all that is endearing to humanity, by exercising it in the speculation and practice of the virtues, is the most godlike occupation, and the great purpose of moral precept and sound philosophy.

GENERAL WASHINGTON was in his person about six feet in height, his eyes were gray, but full of animation : his visage was serene, and the temper of his thoughtful mind did not seem disposed to the frequent indulgence of mirth ; his limbs were well proportioned and muscular, and his deportment carried an air of majesty and solemnity in it, that was altogether awful to folly : though no man did more for the interests of human nature in general, yet few men have unbosomed themselves with more circumspection than he did, to any particular individual ; but this habit of reserve has been the characteristic of the wisest persons that ever lived, when possessed of similar authority—it has been asserted that he was never seen to smile, during the progress of the revolutionary war : in the more unrestrained moments of private intercourse, he expressed himself with perspicuity and diffidence, but seldom used more words than were necessary for the elucidation of his opinion: the lineaments of his face implied that he was an older man than he really was ; but the weight of care, that must necessarily have pressed upon the reflection of a man, engaged in such a continuity of vast enterprize and deep responsibility, could not fail to antedate in some degree, the works of time.

THE graces of General WASHINGTON's person, were not unfrequently instrumental in the promotion of his views ; the advantages resulting from natural grace, in polished and even savage life, are wonderfully convictive ; and this effect will not be amazing, when it is known, that the most penetrating analyzers of man, and his attributes, have determined that all action is graceful, in proportion as the impulses are innocent : nothing that is vicious or abominable can be charming : nor does it breathe or exist in any emotions arising from vanity or folly : grace is the sublimity of beauty : it is a quality analagous to the most exquisite tenderness of affection ; that modest, yet gay illustration of action, which accompanies

z

pure love : gracefulness is an expression of dignified pleasure ; but that high order of pleasure is not ease, it is something more.

AS a didactic writer, he can scarcely be esteemed too much ; his sentiments have a force and fascination to restore reason, invigorate patriotism, and awaken piety : his public letters and documents should be engraved upon the tablet of the nation, as examples of profound sagacity, genuine integrity, and unaffected humility : they should be eternally regarded, in a political interpretation, as " eyes to the blind" : his simplicity of style proves him to have been guided by a fine taste ; when a writer is verbose or glittering, his argument is weakened, and none but the unwise can admire him.

IT was the peculiar honour of General WASHINGTON, not only to deserve, but to enjoy the approbation of all men of probity in either hemisphere ; those persons who had been his opponents in Britain, from an attachment to their sovereign and the prevailing councils of the hour, became his friends at the conclusion of a peace, from

contemplating the moderation of his deportment, and the moral energies of his mind ;
and some of the more distinguished, considered it as a reflected merit, to be in the habits of correspondence and the interchange of
civilities,* with such an embellished and ad-
mirable personage.

HE had the urbanity of a gentleman,
without the littlenesses of pride ; and in the
very plenitude of his authority, would
sheathe a denial so kindly, that the sting of
disappointment was absorbed in the beauty
of the declaration : he embraced the delegation to rule, as a great man should ; not to
indulge the luxury of the senses, or the in-

---

* *Item*, To the *Earl of Buchan* I recommit " the Box made
of the oak that sheltered the great Sir *William Wallace*, after the
battle of Falkirk"—presented to me by his lordship, in terms too
flattering for me to repeat, with a request " to pass it, on the event
of my decease, to the man in my country, who should appear to
merit it best, upon the same conditions that have induced him to
send it to me." Whether easy or not, to select *the man* who might
comport with his lordship's opinion in this respect, is not for me
to say ; but conceiving that no disposition of this valuable curiosity can be more eligible than the recommitment of it to his
own cabinet, agreeably to the original design of the Goldsmiths'
company of Edinburgh, who presented it to him, and, at his request, consented that it should be transferred to me—I do give
and bequeath the same to his lordship ; and, in case of his decease, to his heir, with my grateful thanks for the distinguished
honour of presenting it to me, and more especially for the favourable sentiments with which he accompanied it.
(*Washington's Will.*)

satiate aims of ambition, but for the blessed
purpose of disseminating love and protection to all : he stood as a preeminent sup-
porter in society ; like a Tuscan column,
with sober magnificence ; plain, strong, at-
tractive and erect : with Atlantean proper-
ties, equal to more than the weight he had
sustained : at once the vital principle and
the ornament of that constitution he had
sanctioned, and his fame will be co-eternal
with the existence of freedom.

WE have never contemplated the character of a magistrate more inflexible to wrong,
nor of a man so active and so spotless, in
any record, either antient or modern : he
did more for imitation, and less for repen-
tance, than any contemporary : had he derived his ideas of legislation and forbearance
from the statutes of the golden age, he
could not have done more to enforce innocency
and mutual truth ; and he confessedly lived
to make mankind better, if it is in the virtue of an individual to correct our frailty.

HAVING followed this august statesman
to the sepulchre, it now devolves upon the
grateful and the provident of his country-

men, to hang it round with symbols of regard;and inscribe it with the texts of his policy : let them inform a future age, that he
shunned no public question, nor omitted
any duty ; in the cherishing hope, that other
men may copy the impressive example : and
the insinuation of hope makes our delusion
our joy ; but, in simplicity, yet force, of
language : in clearness of understanding
and depth of judgment : in his disdain of
any commutation with falshood : in his
contempt of trivial expedients, and his ability to make that spirit governing : in his
appropriation of direct remedies for national
evils, and in his majesty of character altogether, we have seriously to apprehend that
he will be never equalled ; he had all the
decision of *Cato*, without his coarseness—he
had raised himself, by progressive excellence,
above the tooth of envy, and the despera-
tion of malice : and was not assailable by
any mortal hand :

> ———Nec Jovis ira, nec ignes,
> Nec poterit ferrum, nec edax abolere vetustas.
>
> Ovid, Metam. lib. 15.

HE is now removed from terrestrial vicissitudes and the incorrigibility of folly forever ; and is sainted in heaven, if it is in

the piety of a people to canonize their benefactor : he was a rare luminary, as mild as
he was effulgent, and, we trust, that the influence of his bright example will be coeval
with our nation : he approached as nearly
to the divine essence, as any thing human
can. Let those (if such there are) who,from
depravity of intellect, or imbecility of mind,
may think of General WASHINGTON with ir-
reverence, reflect maturely upon what America might have been, had not such a preserver
been among us. When the varied beauties of
legislation lay before him, he recommended
those articles for congressional adoption,
which were most analogous to our habits,
and best suited for our prosperity : liberty
is less endangered here, than in any other
country, as there is more general intelligence
in the community : those overheated zeal-
ots, who may believe that he did not do
enough, are but imperfectly acquainted with
the assimilation of principle and practice :
we can fondly transfer a theory from our
fancy to our expectation, that would be
ephemeral in execution : the doctrines
which are fulminated by enthusiasm, must
be tried by experience and mellowed by wis-

dom, before the statute can be properly operative : those laws sustain public virtue the longest, which are reconcileable to moderation and the floating usages of civil life : this is not an epoch of romance, and all utopian follies should be exploded : we may demand much for common comfort, but we must yield something to insure its continuation.

[IT was originally intended, by the compilers of this work, to have omitted the celebrated anonymous letter, written by an officer of the American army, encamped near New Windsor, in March, 1783;—but they have been induced to insert it as a necessary preface to, the inimitable answer of the commander in chief; who, it has been suggested by some friends of high political reputation, had never, on any occasion, discovered a superior promptitude of talent, and dexterity of address, than in suppressing the deep laid mischief of this ingenious incendiary, whose insidious eloquence had almost inflamed to revolt the then untainted purity of American valour.

[IT may be proper before we give this artful letter, to state further, that a memorial was presented to Congress, in Dec. 1782, in behalf of the army, by three commissioners, consisting of Maj. Gen. *M'Dougall*, and two field officers, in which their wishes were thus expressed: " 1. present pay.—2. a settlement of the arrearages of pay, and security for what is due.—3. a commutation of the half pay allowed by different resolutions of Congress for an equivalent in gross.—4. a settlement of the account of deficiences of rations and compensations.—5. a settlement of the accounts of deficiences of cloathing and compensation." In April following, the army was informed, by their Commissioners, that Congress had " decided on nothing of moment for them." Upon this, a meeting of the general and field officers was called, at the public building, for the express purpose of considering " what further measures (if any) should be adopted to obtain redress." This anonymous summons was accompanied with the letter in question.]

TO THE OFFICERS OF THE ARMY.

GENTLEMEN,

A FELLOW soldier, whose interest and affections bind him strongly to you, whose past sufferings has been as great, and whose future fortunes may be as desperate as yours—would beg leave to address you.

AGE has its claims, and rank is not without its pretensions to advise, but though unsupported by both, he flatters himself, that the plain language of sincerity and experience, will neither be unheard nor unregarded.

LIKE many of you, he loved private life, and left it with regret. He left it, determined to retire from the field, with the necessity that called him to it, and not till then— not till the enemies of his country, the slaves of power, and the hirelings of injustice, were compelled to abandon their schemes, and acknowledge America as terrible in arms as she had 'been humble in remonstrance. With this object in view, he has long shared in your toils, and mingled in your dangers. He has felt the cold hand of poverty without a murmur, and has seen the growing insolence of wealth without a sigh.—But, too much under the direction of his wishes, and sometimes weak enough to take desire for opinion, he has till lately, very lately, believed in the justice of his country. He hoped that as the clouds of adversity scattered, and as the sunshine of peace and better fortune broke in upon us, the coldness and severity of government would relax, and that, more than justice, that gratitude, would blaze forth upon those hands, which had upheld her in the darkest stages of her passage, from impending servitude to acknowledged independence. But faith has its limits as well as temper, and there are points beyond which neither can be stretched, without sinking into cowardice, or plunging into credulity. This, my friends, I conceive to be your situation. Hurried to the very verge of both, another step would ruin you forever. To be tame and unprovoked when injuries press hard upon you, is more than weakness; but to look up for kinder usage, without one manly effort of your own, would fix your character, and shew the world how richly you deserve those chains you broke. To guard against this evil, let us take a view of the ground upon which we now stand, and thence carry our thoughts forward, for a moment, into the unexplored field of expedient.

AFTER a pursuit of seven years, the object for which you set out is at length brought within your reach. Yes, my friends, that suffering courage of yours, was active once ; it has conducted the United States of America through a doubtful and bloody war. It has placed her in the chair of independency, and peace returns again to bless—whom? A country courting your return to private life, with tears of gratitude, and smiles of admiration. Longing to divide with you that independency which your gallantry has given, and those riches which your wounds have preserved ? is this the case ? or is it rather, a country that tramples upon your rights, disdains your cries, and insults your distresses ? have you not, more than once, suggested your wishes, and made known your wants to Congress ? wants and wishes which gratitude and policy should have anticipated, rather than evaded. And have you not lately in the meek language of intreating memorials, begged from their justice, what you could no longer expect from their favour ? how have you been answered ? let the letter which you are called to consider to-morrow make the reply.

IF this then be your treatment, while the swords you wear are necessary for the de-

fence of America, what have you to expect
from peace when your voice shall sink, and
your strength dissipate by division ? when
those very swords, the instruments and
companions of your glory shall be taken
from your sides, and no remaining mark of
military distinctions be left, but your marks,
infirmities, and scars ? can you then consent
to be the only sufferers by this revolution,
and, retiring from the field, grow old in poverty, wretchedness, and contempt ? can you
consent to wade through the vileness of de-
pendency, and owe the miserable remains of
life to charity, which has hitherto been spent
in honour !—if you can—go—and carry with
you the jest of tories, and the scorn of
whigs ; the ridicule, and what is worse, the
pity of the world.   Go, starve, and be forgotten ! but if your spirit should revolt at
this ; if you have sense enough to discover,
and spirit sufficient to oppose tyranny, whatever garb it may assume ; whether it be the
plain coat of republicanism, or the splendid
robe of royalty ; if you have yet learned to
discriminate between a people and a cause ;
between men and principles—awake—attend
to your situation, and redress yourselves.
If the present moment be lost, every future

effort is in vain ; and your threats then will
be as empty as your entreaties now.

I WOULD advise you, therefore, to come
to some final opinion, upon what you can
bear, and what you will suffer. If your determination be in any proportion to your
wrongs, carry your appeal from the justice
to the fears of government. Change the
milk and water style of your memorials ; assume a bolder tone ; decent, but lively, spirited, and determined ; and suspect the man
who would advise to more moderation, or
longer forbearance. Let two or three men
who can feel as well as write, be appointed
to draw up your late remonstrance ; for I
would no longer give it the soothing, soft,
unsuccessful epithet of memorial.—Let it represent, in language that will neither dishonour you by its rudeness, nor betray you by
its fears, what has been promised by Congress, and what has been performed ; how
long and how patiently you have suffered—
how little you have asked ; and how much
of that little has been denied. Tell them
that, though you were the first, and would
wish to be the last to encounter danger : that
though despair itself can never drive you in-

to dishonour, it may drive you from the
field; that the wound often irritated, and
never healed, may at length become incura-
ble—and that the slightest mark of indignity
from Congress now, must operate like the
grave, and part you forever—that in any
political event, the army has its alternative.
If peace, that nothing shall separate you
from your arms but death.   If war, that
courting the auspices, and inviting the direction of your illustrious leader, you will
retire to some yet unsettled country, smile
in your turn, and "mock when their fear
cometh on."   But let it represent also, that
should they comply with the request of your
late memorials, it would make you more
happy, and them more respectable.—That
while the war should continue, you would
follow their standard to the field ; and that
when it came to an end, you would withdraw into the shade of private life, and give
the world another subject of wonder and applause ;—an *army victorious over its enemies—
victorious over itself.*

[IMMEDIATELY on the circulation of the foregoing address, the commander in chief issued an official order, convening the general and field officers at the new building, to hear the report of the commissioners from the army to Congress, and to devise what further measures ought to be adopted, as the most rational, and best calculated to attain the just and important object in view. In this meeting, which was fully attended by the general and field officers, by one officer from each company, and by a suitable representation of the staff—the commander in chief thus addressed the army :]

GENTLEMEN,

By an anonymous summons, an attempt has been made to convene you together. How inconsistent with the rules of propriety, and how subversive of all order and discipline, let the good sense of the army judge !

In the moment of this summons, another anonymous production was put into circulation, addressed more to the feelings and passions than to the reason and judgment of the army. The author of the piece is intitled to much credit for the goodness of his pen ; and I could wish he had as much credit for the rectitude of his heart ; for, as men see through difficulties, and are induced by the reflecting faculties of the mind, to use dif-

ferent means to attain the same end, the author of the piece should have had more
charity than to mark for suspicion, the man
who should recommend moderation and
longer forbearance, or, in other words, who
should not think as he thinks, and act as he
advises.   But he had another plan in view,
in which candour and liberality of sentiment,
regard to justice, and love of country, have
no part ; and he was right to insinuate the
darkest suspicions to effect the blackest designs.   That the address is drawn with great
art ; that it is intended to answer the most
insidious purposes ; that it is intended to
impress the mind with an idea of premedi-
tated injustice to the sovereign power of the
United States, and rouse all those resent-
ments which must unavoidably flow from
such a belief ; that the first mover of this
scheme, whoever he may be, intended to
take advantage of the passions, while they
were warmed with the recollection of past
distresses, without giving time for cool deliberate thinking, and that composure of
mind which is necessary to give dignity and
stability to measures, is rendered too obvi-

ous, by the mode of conducting the business, to need other proof than a reference to the proceeding.

THUS much, gentlemen, I have thought it incumbent on me to observe to you, to shew upon what principles I opposed the hasty, irregular meeting which was proposed to be held on Tuesday last, and not because I wanted a disposition to give you every opportunity, consistent with your own honour, and the dignity of the army to make known your grievances. If my conduct heretofore, has not evinced to you, that I have been a faithful friend to the army, my declaration of it at this time would be equally unavailing and improper. But as I was among the first who embarked in the cause of our common country, as I have never left your side one moment, but when called from you on public duty ; as I have been the constant companion and witness of your distresses, and not amongst the last to feel and acknowledge your merits ; as I have ever considered my own military reputation as inseparably connected with that of the army ; and my heart has ever expanded with joy, when I heard its praises, and my indignation has risen, when the mouth of detraction has been opened against it, it can scarcely be supposed at this last stage of the war, that I am indifferent to its interests. But how are they to be promoted? the way is plain, says the anonymous addresser. "If war continues, remove into the unsettled country, there establish yourselves, and leave an ungrateful country to defend itself." But whom are they to defend? our wives, our children, and our farms, and other property which we have left behind us? or in this state of hostile separation, are we to take the two first (the latter cannot be removed) to perish in a wilderness with hunger, cold, and nakedness? If peace takes place, " never sheathe your swords," says he, " until you have obtained full and ample justice." This dreadful alternative of either deserting our country in the extremest hour of her distress, or turning our arms against it, which is the apparent object, unless Congress can be compelled into instant compliance, has something so shocking in it, that humanity revolts at the idea. My God! what can this writer have in view, by recommending such measures? can he be a friend to the army ? can he be a friend to the country ? rather is he not an insidious foe ? some emissary, perhaps, from Newyork, plotting the ruin of both, by sowing the seeds of discord and separation between the civil and military powers of the continent ? and what a compliment does he pay to our understandings, when he recommends measures, in either alternative, impracticable in their nature ? but here, gentlemen, I will drop the curtain, because it would be as imprudent in me to assign my reasons for this opinion, as it would be insulting to your conception, to suppose you stood in need of them. A moment's reflection will convince every dispassionate mind of the physical impossibility of carrying either project into execution. There might, gentlemen, be an impropriety in my taking notice, in this address to you, of an anonymous production ; but the manner in which this performance has been introduced to the army, the effect it was intended to have, together with some other circumstances, will amply justify my observations upon the tendency of that writing.

WITH respect to the advice given by the author, to suspect the man who shall recommend moderation and longer forbearance, I spurn it, as every man who regards that liberty and reveres the justice for which we contend, undoubtedly must ; for, if men are to be precluded from offering their sentiments on a matter which may involve the consideration of mankind, reason is of no use to us. The freedom of speech may be taken away, and dumb and silent we may be led, like sheep to the slaughter. I cannot in justice to my own belief, and which I have great reason to believe is the intention of Congress, conclude this address, without giving it as my decided opinion, that that honorable body entertain exalted sentiments of the services of the army, and from full conviction of its merits and sufferings, will do it complete justice : that their endeavours to discover and establish funds, have been unwearied, and will not cease till they have succeeded, I have not a doubt.

BUT like all other large bodies, where there is a variety of different interests to reconcile, their deliberations are slow. Why then should we distrust them ? and in consequence of that distrust, adopt measures which would cast a shade over that glory

which has been so justly acquired, and tarnish the reputation of an army which has
been celebrated through all Europe for its
fortitude and patriotism? and for what is
this done ? to bring the object we seek for
nearer ? no, most certainly, in my opinion, it will cast it at a greater distance. For
myself, and I take no merit in giving the assurance, being induced to it from principles
of gratitude, veracity, and justice, a grateful
sense of the confidence you have ever placed
in me, a recollection of the cheerful assistance and prompt obedience I have experienced from you, under every vicissitude of
fortune, and the sincere affection I feel for
an army I had so long the honour to command, will oblige me to declare in this public and solemn manner, that in the attainment of complete justice for all your toils
and dangers, and in the gratification of every wish, so far as may be done consistently
with the great duty I owe my country, and
those powers I am bound to respect, you
may freely command my services to the utmost of my abilities.

WHILE I give you these assurances and
pledge myself in the most unequivocal man-

ner to exert whatever ability I am possessed
of in your favour, let me entreat you, gentlemen, on your part, not to take any measures, which, viewed in the calm light of
reason, will lessen the dignity and sully the
glory you have hitherto maintained.—Let
me request you to rely on the plighted faith
of your country, and place a full confidence
in the purity of the intentions of Congress,
that previous to your dissolution, as an army, they will cause all your accounts to be
fairly liquidated, as directed in the resolutions which were published to you two days
ago, and that they will adopt the most effectual measures in their power to render ample justice to you, for your faithful and mer-
itorious services. And let me conjure you
in the name of our common country, as you
value your own sacred honour, as you respect the sacred rights of humanity, and as
you regard the military and national character of America to express your utmost horror and detestation of the man, who wishes, under any specious pretences, to overturn
the liberties of our country, and who wick-
edly attempts to open the floodgates of civil
discord, and deluge our rising empire with
blood.

BY thus determining, and thus acting, you will pursue the plain and direct road to the attainment of your wishes ; you will defeat the insidious designs of your enemies, who are compelled to resort from open force to secret artifice. You will give one more proof of unexampled patriotism and patient virtue, rising superior to the pressure of the most complicated sufferings ; and you will by the dignity of your conduct, afford occasion for posterity to say, when speaking of the glorious example you have exhibited to mankind, " had this day been wanting, the world had never seen the last stage of perfection to which human nature is capable of attaining."

GEORGE WASHINGTON.

Head Quarters, Newburgh,
    March 15, 1783.

[HIS excellency the commander in chief having withdrawn, the following resolutions were moved by generals *Knox* and *Putnam*, and adopted by the meeting :—" *Resolved*, that the unanimous thanks of the officers of the army, be presented to the commander in chief for his excellent address, and the communications he has been pleased to make to them ; and to assure him, that the officers reciprocate his affectionate expressions, with the greatest sincerity of which the human heart is capable :"—" *Resolved*, that at the commencement of the war, the officers of the American army engaged in the service of their country from the purest love and attachment to the rights and liberties of human nature ; which motive still exists in the highest degree ; and that no circumstance of distress or danger, shall induce a conduct that may tend to sully the reputation and glory which they have acquired, at the price of their blood, and eight years faithful service."—" *Resolved*, that the army continue to have an unshaken confidence in the virtue of Congress, and their country."—" *Resolved*, that the officers of the American army, view with abhorrence, and reject with disdain, the infamous propositions contained in a late anonymous address to them, and resent with indignation the secret attempts of some unknown person to collect the officers together, in a manner totally subversive of all discipline and good order."]

SUBSCRIBERS' NAMES.

BOSTON.

ANDREWS John
Abbot Samuel
Andrews William
Ayers Nathaniel
Amory Thomas
Adams Jofeph
Avery John jun.
Allen & Tucker
Atherton A. H.
Auftin Jofeph
Ames Jonas
Ames Aaron
Andrews James
Appleton George W.
Aiken Jofeph
Amory John jun.
Allen Jeremiah efq
Andrews John efq..
Allen James A.
Archbald Thomas G.
Appleton Samuel
Adams Abraham jun.
Amory Thomas C. 2
Appleton Nathaniel
Buffey Benjamin
Barrel Jofeph efq.
Bulfinch Charles
Brewfter Oliver
Bromfield Henry
Blake Thomas
Burchfted James
Bridge Jofeph
Briggs Enos jun.
Blake Martin
Bingham Caleb 6
Burge Jofeph
Bowen Daniel
Barrett G. L. 4
Bafs Henry jun,
Burbeck John
Briggs Thomas
Bowen Nathaniel
Bulfinch Samuel

Blake George efq 2
Brooks P. C.
Bordman W. H.
Bordman W. jun.
Bridge Matthew
Brewe Thomas
Blanchard J. W.
Brindley Francis
Bradlee Samuel
Battelle Timothy
Barrett George
Brailsford Norton
Bates Daniel 4
Brimmer Herman
Blackburn Abner
Butterfield Abraham
Balch Jonathan
Babcock Adam 2
Bowdoin James efq. 2
Bacon Jofiah
Bridge Samuel
Barrel Jofeph jun.
Bowers Samuel
Bryant Abel
Blanchard George
Bumftead Jeremiah jun.
Baynes John 2
Broaders Prifcilla
Bowers Phineas
Bazin Abraham
Baker John
Bowman Edmund
Bradlee John
Bradlee Thomas
Bradford William
Badger Daniel
Bazin John
Bacon Robert
Bixby Luther
Boot & Pratt
Bright George
Barnes Benjamin
Billings Samuel
Boardman Darius

Benn Abraham
Brown William
Brown Jofiah
Burley Thomas 2
Bradbury Charles
Blake Edward jun.
Blanchard John
Bradlee Jofiah
Bigelow Afahel
Baker Luke
Burroughs George efq.
Brewer James
Boit Henry
Boot Francis
Bradford L.
Child David
Crocker Samuel M.
Copeland Nathaniel
Chamberlaine Richard
Coverly Samuel
Clark George
Callender Jofeph
Callender William
Carnes John
Cooper Samuel
Collins John
Church Edward
Cruft Hannah
Campbell James
Cufhing Henry
Clark Humphrey
Crocker Mathias
Clark Nathaniel
Creafe John
Creafe Samuel
Clark Simpfon
Crosby Joel
Coates Benjamin
Carney Daniel
Clark Willard
Cotting U.
Codman Stephen
Coolidge Cornelius

Cufhing Samuel
Crane Abijah
Carter John
Cravath Lemuel
Callender Thomas
Cockran William   2
Chapman Jofeph
Crocker Allen
Cleland William
Codman John
Cook Ifrael
Clarke Samuel
Cornwall J. G.
Clarke John
Cazneau Edward jun.
Callender Benjamin
Cunningham Robert
Calleuder Jofeph jun.
Cordis Thomas
Cufhing John
Campbell James
Clark Thomas
Cooper Samuel efq.
Cobb Benjamin
Curtis Thomas
Cunningham George
Clapp William
Dolliver Peter
Dow Weare
Dennie Thomas   2
Dexter Doct. Aaron
Davies Lucy
Dehon William
Dinfmore William
Duick Benjamin
Doyle W. M. S.
Davis Thomas efq.
Davis Eliphalet
Davenport Addington 2
Dix Jofeph
Dickinfon Thomas efq 2
Delano Benjamin
Downes Lydia
Dorr Jofeph H.
Dewhurft Henry
Dench Lawfon
Dyer Jeremiah
Dyer John D.
Dawfon James
Davenport Samuel D.

Davis Amafa
Drew Job
Durant Cornelius
Davis Charles
Davis Jofhua
Duncan Lt. G. W.
Evans Robert
Eaton William B.
Ellis Jabez
Elliot Rev, John D. D.
Emmons Nathaniel
Emerfon Rev. W.
Ellifon James
Ellifon William jun.
Elliot Maj. G. Simon 2
Emes Luther
Fofdick Jofeph
Fox John
Farley Abel
Fitch Jeremiah
Freeman Nathaniel
Freeman Watfon
Farley Ebenezer
Feffenden Benj. jun.
Fofter Nathaniel   2
Freeman Conftant
Fofter James H.
Fleet John jun.
Farnum Rufus
Fowle Jofiah
Furnefs W lliam
Fales & Keith
Fuller Stephen jun.
Farwell Oliver
Freeman Rowland
Fielden Thomas
Farmer William
Fofter Jofeph
Foxcroft Jofeph E.
Fofter James
Field Jofeph
Francis Ebenezer
Fowle Henry
Furber Thomas
Gardner Samuel efq.
Goldfbury Samuel   2
Guirey Nitham
Gilbert John
Godfrey Thomas
Gore Stephen

Goodale Nathan
Goodale Amos
Gooch James   2
Goddard Nathaniel   3
Greenwood W. P.
Greenleaf Thomas
Geyer J. W.   5
Gair Jofeph
Gorham Stephen efq. 3
Gray S.
Gray Edward jun.
Hall Jofeph efq.
Hurd Jofeph
Howe Thomas
Harris Leach
Hammatt H. H.   2
Homer Andrew
Hawkins Samuel
Harris William
Homes Barzillai
Hawkins Benjamin 12
Homer Benjamin
Hubbard Henry
Herring Ebenezer
Haftings Jofeph S.
Haftings Thomas
Harris John
Hunnewell Jonathan 2
Hewes Thomas   2
Hyde Jofhua
Harris Jofeph
Hufe Enoch
Holden William
Hammond Afa
Hamock Charles
Hinkley Abigail
Hearfey John
Hatch Ifrael
Homer William
Hale John
Hunt Mathew M.
Hoffman John
Hagger Benjamin K.
Hagger Jonas
Hale Timothy
Hawkes Levi
Hitchborn Benjamin
Haven William
Hammatt John B.
Homes Robert

Poor Moses
Parfons Eben jun.
Rowe Hannah 2
Rich Obadiah jun.
Ruft William
Ruggles Samuel
Richardfon William
Rice John
Richards Nathaniel
Runey Robert
Read Jofeph
Ripley Jofeph
Richards Jofeph
Renaud A.
Ruffell Jofeph efq. 2
Rogers Daniel D.
Rowe Jofeph
Richards Elizabeth
Revere Jofhua
Rogers S.
Read Sampfon
Roulftone Michael
Roberts Jofiah
Rand doct. Ifaac
Richardfon Jeffrey
Smith George
Storer Ebenezer efq.
Sears David 4
Spooner doct. William
Sullivan James efq.
Sigourncy Elifha
Scollay William
Shimmin William
Smith N.
Sawyer Artemas
Smith Samuel 2
Sargent capt. Daniel 2
Sargent Maj. John T. 2
Sumner Benjamin
Smith William
Sturgis Ruffell efq.
Sumner Samuel
Sigourney Andrew
Snow Jofhua
Stedman Jofiah
Swan Jofhua
Symmes Ebenezer
Stackpole William 2
Salifbury Samuel 2
Scholtz John G.

Simonds Benjamin
Swett Samuel
Sewall Jofeph
Story William
Swan Thomas
Smith Adam
Scudder Daniel
Sturgis Samuel
Stutfon Samuel
Snow Prince jun.
Singleton James C.
Salter Richard
Smith John
Seaver Nathaniel
Smith & Turner
Sanger Jeffee
Simmons Thomas
Sigourney Daniel
Skinner William S.
Smith Benjamin jun.
Salifbury S. jun.
Sullivan J, L.
Stoddard David
Thayer Minot
Thwing Samuel jun.
Thompfon Jofiah
Tichnor Elifha
Townfend David
Tucker & Thayer 2
Tuckerman Guftavus
Tyler David
Tuckerman Edward jr.
Tucker Beza
Torrey Jofeph
Tilefton Lemuel
Tyler Ifaac
Trott Andrew C.
Thayer Amafa
Tuck Samuel G.
Treat Robert
Tucker Richard D.
Tyler Jofeph
Thayer David
Tilden Jofeph jun.
Thayer Maj. S. M.
Tilden B. L.
Taylor John
Turner William
Tudor William efq.
Tillotfton Daniel

Thomas doct. Jofhua
Tufts Ebenezer
Thayer Nathaniel
Thayer Mofes
Thayer Richard
Thayer John
Thwing James
Vofe Betfey E
Vinton Jofiah jun.
Vofe Charles
Voax Thomas
Varney Benjamin
Vofe Jofhua
Vollentine Nathaniel
Whitney Amos
Whiting George
Watfon George 2
Wakefield Terence
Waters John
Waters J. jun.
Wells Seth
Welch John N.
Wells Arnold jun. 2
Watfon Marfton 3
Whiting Ruggles
Winthrop John jun,
Wells Benjamin T.
Webb Nathan
Wheelwright Job
Webfter Redford
Welfh doct. Thomas
Wade Ebenezer 2
Woodward Smith
Weld Daniel
Willard Jofiah
Williams Thomas
Weft Nathaniel P.
Whitman Davis
Wright Edmund
Winthrop Thomas L.
Wiggin Benjamin
White Ebenezer 3
Wilington Jonathan
Winflow gen. Jôhn
Wild Abraham
Warren doct. John
Winfhip Amos
Wells Ebenezer
White Ifaac
White Cornelius

Whitwell William
Whipple doct. Jofeph
Winfhip Stephen
Whitney Ezra 2
Wait John
Wheeler Mofes
Williams John D. 2

SALEM.

Appleton William
Andrews Jonathan jun.
Afhton Richard
Allen capt. Edward jun
Appleton John
Barker John
Boden William jun.
Brooks Samuel
Barnes Thomas jun.
Blackler John C.
Beckford Ebenr. efq
Bacon Jacob
Beckford Anne
Barnes James jun.
Barr Robert
Briggs Enos
Blanchard Benjamin
Blanchard Samuel
Bentley Rev. W.
Buffington Capt. John
Bancroft William
Beckford Jonathan
Bigelow William
Buffum Samuel
Buffum Jofhua
Burrill Alden
Butman Eliphalet
Bray Daniel
Burnham John
Barnard Thomas
Babbidge J.
Bacon William
Boit John
Cabot William
Crofs George C.
Crofs Jofeph
Crowninfhield captC 2
Clark John 3d
Cleaveland W. jun.
Collins Tracy

Curwan Samuel
Clark Daniel
Cleaveland Charles
Clark capt. Henry
Carpenter Benjamin
Carnes capt. Jonathan
Collins capt John
Chandler John
Daland Thorndike jun.
Daland John
Dodge Pickering
Dean George
Derby John
Dodge Ifrael jun.
Dodge Benjamin
Derby E. H.
Fogg Jofeph
Felt Benjamin
Felt G. W.
Frye Daniel
Forrefter capt, Simon
Fenno Jofeph
Fairfield capt. John
Fofter capt. John
Gwinn Thaddeus
Goud James
Gray Samuel jun.
Grafton Jofhua
Gray John
Gardner capt. John
Gray William S.
Grafton capt. W.
Glover John
Hiller Jofeph
Hobart Noah
Harvy Amos
Harrington Elifha
Haufter George
Hafhorne Jofeph
Hawks Benjamin
Ingerfol capt. J.
Jeffry James
Johnfon Micajah
Jenks John
King James
Knight Elifha
Lambert Samuel
Lang Dr. E. S.
Laurence capt. Abel

Lander capt. Benjamin
Lander capt. Peter
Lee Thomas jun.
Motey John
Merriam William
Maxey Levi
Mafon capt. Jona. jun.
Manning Rich'd. jun.
Nichols David
Nichols capt. Ichabod
Neill capt John
Osborn Stephen
Ofgood Jofeph
Orne capt William 2
Ofgood Ifaac efq.
Orne Jofiah
Oliver W. W. 3
Ofgood capt John
Pickman Benja. efq. 3
Pritchard John
Prince Henry
Peirce capt. Daniel
Putnam Samuel efq
Pickman Wm efq 2
Page capt Daniel
Plummer Erneftus A
Putnam Barth'w. efq
Putnam capt John
Proctor capt Daniel 2
Putnam Ebenezer
Porter Dudley
Prince capt John jun
Peele capt Jonathan
Perkins Jofeph efq
Peabody capt Jofeph
Peirce Jerathmeel
Perkins capt Thomas
Peirce Nathan
Poole Ward
Ropes Samuel
Richardfon Jofiah
Read Daniel
Ruft capt Henry
Ropes David
Reed Nathan
Ruffell John
Richardfon capt. Wm.
Richardfon Jeffe
Seobie John

Saunders John P
Seccombe Joseph
Seccombe C B
Seccombe Ebenezer
Seccombe Thomas
Seccombe John
Southwick John
Smith Jonathan
Stoddard Ebed
Sumner B. C.
Saunderson Jacob
Sprague Joseph jun
Saunders capt D.
Shillaber Ebenezer
Savage Ezekiel
Smith Elisha
Sprague Joseph esq
Saunders Thomas
Silsbee capt Nathan.
Swett capt Enoch
Sawyer James
Sargent capt F. W.
Sargent capt Ignatius
Saville James
Somes John 3d
Somes capt Benjamin
Saywood William
Somes Isaac
Saywood Daniel
Stephens Cyrus
Sawyer Abraham
Saywood c pt Henry
Turell W. B.
Teague Nathaniel
Tucker Gideon
Treadwell John esq
Ward William
Winn Joseph
Wiggins Richard
Woodbury Josiah
Wiggins Joseph
West capt Benjamin
Webb capt Stephen
Ward Samuel
Ward G. H.
Waters capt Joseph
West capt Nathaniel
Waldo Jonathan esq
Watkins Benjamin
Webb Michael

White capt Edward
West capt Joseph
2 Ward Edward C.

GLOUCESTER.

Allen Joseph jun.
Bates capt, Henry
Brown Elisha
Baker Thomas
Brown Jonathan
Burnham Aaron
Boynton John
Brown Jonathan 3d
Baker Joseph
Butler John
Burnham Ebenezer
Babion William jun.
Corey Thomas
Chellis Gideon
Collins Daniel esq
Choate Josiah
Choate Adoniram
Collins Nathaniel
Currier Adoniram
Cole Weeden
Cleveland Rev. Eben'r.
2 Coffin Lucy
Coffin W.
Cushing Zenas
Coffin Peter esq
Collins Ebenezer H
Dane William
Dennis John jun
Dane John
Dennison James
Dexter William
Dennis Samuel
Davis capt William
Davis Epes
2 Dennis John
Day James
Dennison Isaac
Davis George
Fudger J G
Foster capt J
Forbes Rev Ely
Foster capt J jun
Farr capt David
Fuller Rev David
Foster Elijah jun

Gee capt William
Griffin Nath.
Goss capt James
Gilbert Samuel
Griffin James
Griffin Oliver
Hayes Daniel
Hodgkins Jacob
Hall Aaron
Hough B K
Hardey Samuel
Harriden David
Haskell Nath
Haskell Zebelon
Haskell Aaron
Haskell Daniel
Haskell Stephen
Haskell capt A
Haskell Moses
Haskell Zebelon jun
Haskell W jun
Haskell capt John
Harriden Joseph
Harriden John
Ingersol Rebecca
Ingalls Joseph
Johnson John
Kingsman William
Kingsbury Aaron
Knight Joseph
Kingsman capt John
Knowlton Nehemiah
Knowlton Moses
Kimball David
Kimball capt Jona.
Lane Jonathan D
Lock Joseph
Lufkin capt David
Low capt Francis
Low John jun
Lane David
Littlehale Richard
Low John 2d
Lincoln Pritchard
Littlehale Joseph
Lincoln E
Low John 3d
Lane W R
Luskin Thomas
Luskin William

Mason John
Moore Thomas
Moore Joseph
Mason Thomas
Millett Thomas jun
Mansfield James
Merchant Daniel
Newman John
Norwood Guftavus
Norwood James
Ober Jonathan
Oakes Thomas
Oakes John jun
Parfons capt Thomas
Proctor Ifaac
Pelham Thomas
Poole Major Mark
Pearce capt David
Prindall Eliakim
Parfons Obed
Parfons capt Sam'l jun
Parfons capt Aaron
Parfons Nath
Pear Andrew
Peirce capt. W· jun.
Peirfon W. efq.
Prindall Eldad
Plumier Aaron
Proctor Benjamin
Phelps Henry
Rowe John efq.
Rogers John
Rogers Timothy
Robbins Phillemore
Ruft capt. John
Rogers William
Rogers capt. C   2
Rogers J. G. efq.
Rowe Maj. John
Rowe William
Sargent David
Sargent Abimelech
Sargent Jonathan
Scott John
Stanwood Zebulun
Steel John
Saville Thomas
Sargent Winthrop
Sargent Guftavus
Smith Jacob

Tucker capt. John
Tucker W. efq.
Tappan capt. J
Wharff capt. Ifaac
Woodbury capt. Jofhua
Wallace David
Whittemore Samuel efq.
Warner Daniel efq.
Wharff capt. David
Warner capt. Nathl.
Webber capt. J.jun.
White capt. Henry
Whittredge O. S.
Whalen Michael
Woodbury Nathaniel
Whittredge Richard
Webber capt. Benja.
Weft Benjamin

PLYMOUTH.

Crandon Benjamin
Cotton Roffeter
Crombie W. jun.
Crandon C.
Drew Benjamin jun.
Drew Lemuel jun.
Duncan David
Davis William
Dunbar John D.
Dike Anthony
Goodwin William
Goodwin Timothy
Holmes El·azer
Hodge Barnabas,jun.
Haywood Nathan
Harlow Southwick
Jackfon William
Jackfon Charles
Jackfon Thomas jun.
Jackfon Johnfon
Janes Samuel
Kendall James
Lothrop Nathaniel
Morton Lemuel
Paty John
Richardfon R R.
Ruffell Nathaniel
Seymour Benjamin.
Spooner Ephraim

Thacher James
Thomas Jofhua
Truft Jofeph
Torrey John
Tufts Jonathan
Weld Jabez & co.
Watfon William
Wethrell Thomas jun.
Whiting Benjamin
Wethrell Thomas

DORCHESTER.

Blackman James
Badlam Ezra
Bowman W. efq.
Baker Edmund
Badlam Stephen jun.
Blake Enos
Crehore Samuel
Clap Samuel
Capen Ebenezer
Clap Jofeph
Davenport Ebenezer
Davenport Samuel
Davenport capt. James
Davenport Daniel
Eaton capt. Pearfon
Everett Mofes
Glover Samuel
Hawes Jeffe
Howe Ifaac
Hall Richard
How Abraham
Hearfey J
Hawes William T.
Jacobs Benjamin
Leeds Daniel A. M.
Lewis James
Leeds Alexander
Peirce Stephen
Prefton John
Peirce col. Samuel
Robinfon James
Robinfon Maj. James
Richards Samuel
Sanderfon Ifaac
Simmons Benjamin
Sumner William
Tilefton Euclid

Tower Daniel
Thayer Arodi
Tolman Ebenezer
Topliff Samuel A. M.
Williams John
Willington Ebenezer
Withington Edward
Withington Samuel
Walker William
Whitney Mofes

MARBLEHEAD.

Bowen Nathan
Bond John
Blacker C W
Barker Jofeph
Boden William
Bartlett Samuel
Duey John
Devereaux Samuel
Elkins Thomas
Gerry Samuel R
Goodwin John
Graves Ebenezer
Hooper William
Hooper Nathaniel
Hooper Robert
Hafkell Thomas
Hooper Samuel
Hooper Benjamin jun.
Lewis Edmund
Lee William R
Lee Samuel
Martin Knott
Mansfield Ifaac
Orne Jofhua
Prentifs Jofhua
Prince Richard
Reed William
Story Ifaac
Story Elifha
Sparhawk John
Tedder John
Wilfon Jofeph
Waite John

WALPOLE, (N. H.)

Allen gen. Amafa
Alker Thomas

Bullard maj. Afa   2
Bellows Jofeph jun
Belcher John
Bennett Mofes
Bellows Rofwell
Bellows Thomas efq
Cunningham John
Chamberlain H V
Drew Thomas C
Elkins Harvey
Feffenden Rev Tho's.
Gardner Francis efq
Lacey Daniel
M'Hurin E H
Redington Thomas
Sturtevant Ifaac
Stone David
Thomas Alexander efq.
Vofe Roger efq.

KEENE, (N H)

Adams Dr Daniel
Blake Abel capt
Blake Solomon
Bond John G   12
Bachelor Thomas P
Blake W W
Cooke Noah efq
Clarke Feffenden
Chapman Daniel
Crofsfield Amos
Dinsmore Samuel efq.
Dorr Jofeph
Eafterbrook John
Edwards Dr. Thomas
Forbes David efq
Hall rev Aaron
Johnfon Mofes
Lamfon William   4
Morfe James
Maccarty D Thad.
Newcomb hon. Daniel
Nims capt Alpheus
Prentifs John
Ralfton James B
Ralfton Alexander efq
Stiles Jeremiah efq
Stiles Jofeph
Todd major William

WISCASSETT

Adams Samuel
Anderfon Francis
Bowman Jonathan jun
Blythe Francis
Bloffom Mathew
Bradford Alden
Child Royland
Crate Thomas M
Danforth Jofhua
Elwell Robert
Foye William jun
Foye John S
Glidden John
Hodge James
Hilton Andrew
Hilton Jofhua
Moffat James
Minot John jun
Pike William
Payfon Jonathan
Stetfon Jofeph
Smith Ebenezer
Sanborn Bradbury
Tinkham Jofeph
Tinkham Seth
Tinkham Spencer
Thayer Zebediah
Woood J T
Wood Abial jun

CONCORD.

Ambrofe Stephen
Abbot Jofeph
Abbot Ephraim
Ayers Richard
Abbot Jacob
Choate Robert
Chandler Timoth
Carrigain Philip jun.
Davis John
Dow Jacob
Emmons Jacob
Flagg Ifaac
Farnum Jofiah
Green Nathaniel
Gain Samuel
Hough George

PORTSMOUTH

Alden Timothy
Adams Nathaniel efq.
Bryard Oliver
Buckminfter Jofeph
Blunt O. C.
Chadbourn Th. jun. 4
Cooper W. S.
Haven Jofeph
Hill John B.
Henderfon James
Ladd Henry
Lunt Thomas
Libbey Jeremiah 3
Maffy George jun.
Peirce Charles 12
Perry Martin 2
Slade John S.
Sims Mark
Tappan Amos
Walker Seth
Wentworth John efq.
Walker William

PROVIDENCE.

Arnold Samuel G.
Arnold James
Anthony Michael
Aborn Samuel jnn.
Aborn Peleg
Brown Obediah
Brown Nicholas
Burgifs Triftram
Burroughs George K.
Butler Samuel jun.
Brume Benjamin
Bafton Henry
Butler Cyrus
Barnes D. L.
Blodget William
Brume Allen
Cufhing Nathaniel
Chaviteau Jofeph
Carlifle Samuel
Clark John J.
Corlis John
Carter John jun.
Carlifle John

Dyer Elifha
Dexter John S.
Dexter Edward
Dorrance John
Eveleth John
Farnum Zebediah
Fifher Nathan
Graves Zephaniah
Green Samuel W.
Halfey T. L. jun
Hitchcock Enos
Hallowell F. A.
Howell J. B.
Jones Gershom
Jones William
Lippett Mofes
Lathrop Zebediah
Lawrence Jofeph
Leonard Ezra jun.
M Lellan Samuel
Mumford John
Macomber Ebenezer
Munroe & co.
Mitchell Mrs.
Mafon Jofeph
Mafon Samuel
Martin Sylvanus G.
Olney Chriftopher
Olney Chriftopher C.
Pick Jofeph
Pick William
Pick Benjamin
Paine Walter
Rhodes Zachariah
Searle Nathaniel
Seamans Young
Smith Benjamin
Snow Warton
Smith Henry
Sheldon Charles
Tingley Araunah
Vinton David
Whipple John
Wheaton Henry
Williams John
Ward John
Wheeler John
Weeden Samuel

PORTLAND.

Bacon Henry
Boyd capt. Jofeph C.
Bagley Abner
Cox John
Frye William R.
Fox Charles
Gregg rev. William
Goodwin Thomas
Harding Arifton
Hopkins James D.
Hunnewel col. Richard
Harper Samuel
Hutfon William
Ilfley Hofea
Ilfley Henry
Jenks Elezer A. 12
Jenks William jun.
Jones Enoch
Johnfon Daniel
Little Charles
Leonard Lieat. Nathl.
Motley Thomas jun.
Moody Benjamin
Moody Nathanl. capt.
Mayo capt. Ebenr.
Moody William
Moody William 2d
Paine Jofiah 6
Peironnet Thomas
Peirfon George
Pratt Nathan
Parker Hon. Ifaac
Poor Frye
Southgate Horatio
Tucker Jofiah
Vaughan William J.
Weeks William C.
Wadfworth John
Woodman John
Waite William
Weeks Lemuel jun.

PITTSFIELD.

Allen Bartlett
Bement H. A.
Larned Simeon

IPSWICH.

Andrews Afa
Burnham Thomas
Baker Afa
Crocker Jofeph
Cogfwell Wade
Caldwell John 3d
Choate David
Coffin Wm. jun.
Dana Jofeph
Dana Samuel
Frifbie Levi
Jewett Richard D.
Kidder Ifaiah
Lord Jofeph
Manning Thomas
Smith Jofhua
Swafey Jofeph
Wallis Mofes
Williams Benjamin

CHARLESTON.

Bartlett Jofiah efq.
Goodwin Edward
Gorham John
Jenkins Ifrael
Jaques Samuel jun,
Lamfon John efq.

NORFOLK, Con.

Aikins Edward
Bartlett Jofeph
Pettibone Auguftus
Robbins Nath
Robbins Thomas

N. PROVIDENCE.

Abbot Stephen
Mafon James
Rhodes Chriftopher
Withington Abraham

STOCKBRIDGE.

Brown Henry
Holbrook E. S.
Ingerfol Jonathan

NEEDHAM.

Bowditch G.
Floyd Philip
Kingfbury Afa
Lyon Peter
Pratt Samuel

DANVERS.

Brown Parker
Endicott John
Fowler Samuel jun.
Gray James
Kettle John
Ofborn Richard
Ofborn Jofeph
Page Samuel
Page John
Putnam Eleazer
Putnam Jeffe
Proctor Sylvefter
Pindar John
Pindar William
Putnam Nathaniel jun.
Poole Fitch
Sprague Jofeph
Storrs Nathaniel
Torrey Jofeph
Willfon Robert

HANOVER.

Brewfter Gen. Eben.
Cabot S. C.
Curtis Col. David
Clark Benjamin
Clark Jofeph
Davis Mofes
Farrar William
Freeman Jonath in
Freeman hon. Ruffell
Gilbert B. I. efq.
Lang Richard
Parks Levi
Stockbridge David
Smith rev. John
Thayer Gideon L.
Woodward maj W.
Woodward Jonathan

ROXBURY.

Ayers Adin
Billing Lemuel
Baker John W.
Dows Thomas
Dudley Jofeph
Davis Aaron
Faxon Elab
Gore Samuel
Gridley James
How James
Lowell Charles
Peirpont Charles
Sumner William H.
Williams Stephen
Wait Samuel
Whiting Joel
Wait Benjamin
Weld Dea. David

TOPSFIELD

Bixby Daniel
Perkins David jun.
Peabody John jun
Perkins Robert jun.
Rogers Joel
Town Jacob 3d
Town David

LEBANON

Billings Stephen
Daken Samuel
Freeman J. O.
Phelps Howard
Wells J. M.

BEVERLY,

Burnham James
Chapman Abner
Endicott Robert
Francis John
Goodrige Samuel
Lee capt. Jofeph
Porter Billy
Thatcher Stephen
Traik Bartholomew
Adams Daniel

Batchelder Nathaniel	*Beverly*	Tibbets John	*Somerſworth*
Brown Benjamin jun.	do	How rev. Perley	*Surry*
Batchelder Joſiah	do	Wheeler J. B.	*Grafton*
Creeſy Henry	do	Farnham Benjamin	*Andover*
Davis Thomas jun.	do	Froſt William	do
Dike John	do	Farrington Philip	do
Foſter Daniel	do	Lovejoy Nathaniel eſq.	do
Furnis William	do	White T. G.	*Wilmington N. C.*
Fiſher Joſhua	do	Storrs Aaron	*Randolph*
Goodridge William	do	Fairchild Timothy	*Norwich*
Giles Ebenezer	do	Williams Joſeph	do
Kilham Abraham	do	Woodward capt. George	do
Lamſon Francis	do	Fry G. Waſhington	*Fryburgh*
Leach Nathan	do	Hubbard Roſwell	*Sulivan*
Leach William jun.	do	Ropes George	*Oxford*
Oliver Jacob	do	Foſter John	*Cambridge*
Packard Ephraim	do	Pomeroy C. W.	do
Stickney Samuel	do	Kingſbury Eliſha	*Alſtead*
Smith Nehemiah	do	Frink Calvin	*Swanſ.y*
Smith Ebenezer jun.	do	Brown Benjamin	do
Stephens John	do	Whitcomb Philemon	do
Thorndike Henry	do	Whitcomb Abijah	do
Thomſon Jacob	do	Foſter Samuel	*Candia*
Treadwell Nathaniel	do	Froſt George	*Northwood*
Thorndike Thomas	do	Froſt John	*Durham*
Whittemore Joſeph	do	Ham John	do
Whitney Eliſha	do	Richardſon Joſeph	do
Wallis Daniel	do	Seywood capt. Henry	do
Whittredge Livermore	do	Foſter Stephen	*Bradford*
Worſley James	od	Greenough Ebenezer.	*Canterbury*
Wallace john	do	Forbes Major Abner	*Wendſor*
Enſlin Frederick	*Boſton*	Grout Benjamin	*Belchertown*
Ellis Jonathan	do	Willard Herman	*Stockbridge*
Eaton David S.	do	Willard John	do
Greene Benjamin jun.	do	Gilman Allen	*Hallowell*
Gridley Richard	do	Greenwood Abel	*Framingham*
Gookin Samuel	do	Gilbert Daniel eſq.	*Enfield*
Glover Lewis	do	Green William	*Medway*
Dow Jabez	*Kenſington*	Hopkins Moſes eſq.	*G. Barrington*
Batchelder Jeremiah	do	Whiting John eſq.	do
Waterman Thomas	*Lebanon*	Hale Enoch	*W. Hampton*
Thayer Ebenezer	*Braintree*	Hall hon. Lott eſq.	*Weſtminſter*
Smith Jacob	*Roylſton*	Traſk capt. Iſrael C.	do
Eaton Jonathan	*Sutton*	Waite Lt. Marmaduke	do
Holmes Heman	*Kingſton*	Herrick Daniel	*Hopkinſton*
Judkins Moſes	do.	Appleton Jeſſe	*Hampton*
Emerſon Edward	*York*	Hyde rev. Alban.	*Lee*
Sewall Daniel eſq.	do	Ingerſol William jun.	do
Froſt William P.	do	Brwer Eliah eſq.	*Lenox*

Gleren Amafa do
Bebee Hofea *N. Canaan*
Barflow Doct Samuel *Sharon*
Bridge Edmund *Drefden* 6
Lithgow J. N. do
Bartlett Jofeph *Stratham*
Hopkins J. *Philadelphia*
Shaw W. H. do.
Butler Benjamin *Deerfield*
Gould Jacob Jun. *Boxford*
Perkins Elifha. do
Kimball Afa do
Symonds Jofeph jun. do
Buxton Samuel *N. Yarmouth*
Brown rev. Clark *Brimfield*
Barrett col. John *Springfield*
Dean Aaron *Charlefton N. H.* 12
Burlin Jepthah *Hopkington*
Bowers Andrew *Salifbury*
Thompfon Thomas do
Wilder Luke do
King John jun. *Abington*
Porter Jacob do
Norton Noah do
Norton William do
Bemis Luke *Watertown*
Faulkner Francis do
Hight William *Berwick*
Pearfon Silas *Newburyport*
Reed Daniel *Lewifton*
Dunning D. *Brunfwick*
Quinbey Henry do
Jenks Nathaniel *N. Gloucefter*
Adams Stephen *Hamilton*
Lukeman Nathan do
Tucker Barnard *Wenham*
Bridge William *Eaft-Sudbury*
Thomas John *Kingfton*
Bigelow Barna *Brookfield*
Snow Gideon *Georgetown*
Brown Jonas efq. *Waltham*
Cufhing Jacob do
Cleaveland Nehemiah *Topsfield*
Dorman Jofeph do
Thaxter rev. Jofeph *M. Vinyard*
Delano Ephraim *Woodwich*
Hill Jeremiah *Biddeford*
Butterfield Erafmus *Malborough*
Stone John do

Vinal capt. W. jun. *Scituate*
Clark Scollo *Weftminfter Ver.*
Dexter Samuel *Wefton*
Bigelow hon. Timothy *Groton*
Dana Samuel do
Prefcott Samuel J. do
Coughran Joel *Jeffry*
Minot Samuel do
Davis Mofes *Edgecombe*
Chaffee Ezra *Newbedford*
Upham Edward *N Salem*
Vofe Solomon efq. *Northfield*
Crocker Samuel *Taunton*
Leonard Apollos B. do
Seabury J. W. do
Crafts David *Manchefter*
Hooper William do
Leach Ezekiel do
Tappan Eben do
Coolidge William *Livermore*
Cook Jofeph efq. *Middlebury*
Chandler John *Petersham*
Carpenter Afahel *Rehoboth*
Ellis James do
Chaviteau J. B. & H. *Havannah*
Chaponel Anthony *Pifcataqua*
Kimball Jacob *Topsfield*
Whitting Nathan *N. Canaan*
Childs Francis *Dedham*
Draper Jofeph do
Greenwood Ifaac do
Harvey Jonathan *Sutton*
Hoit Jofeph B. *Warner*
Leonard Oliver efq *Orrington*
Lucas John *Brooklyne*
Lovejoy Jofhua *Meredith*
Mattoon Ebenezer jun. *Amherft*
M'Clary Michael *Epfon*
Newcomb Richard E. *Greenfield*
Mower Levi *Roylfton Ver.*
Merrill doct. Afa *Lempfter*
Merrit Stephen *Alford*
Nelfon Job. efq. *Cafine*
Norton Samuel *Hingham*
Nelfon Afa *Rowley*
Rofs Donald *Trenton M.* 6
Ofgood Chriftopher *Pembroke*
Porter Jonathan E. *Hadley*
Porter Huntington *Rye*

Vofe Ifaac	*Bofton*	Norton Ichabod	do
Selfridge Thomas O.	do	Kelley Abraham	do
Everett David efq.	do	Coffin James	do
Thomas, Andrews, & Penniman 80	*Albany.*	Coffin Timothy	do
		Olcott Capt. Rofwell	*Norwich*
Athearn capt. W.	*Edgartown*	Parkman J. A.	*Weftborough*
Spalding Rufus	do	Paine Otis	*Foxborough*
Smith Benjamin efq.	do	Peabody Benjamin	*Middleton*
Thaxter Jofeph	do	Peabody Francis	do
Cook Thomas efq.	do	Storrs Seth efq.	do
Jernigam hon. William efq.	do	Stebbs Daniel	do
Athearn hon. James efq.	do	Pinkerton James	*Londonderry*
Cottle Shubael efq.	do	Paine Seth efq.	*Tunbridge*
Tilton Daniel	do	Read Joel	*Attleborough*
Davis Henry	do	Read David	*Smithfield*
Peafe Argalis	do	Ramfey Thomas S.	*Brentwood*
Daggett Timothy	do	Rowfon Mrs	*Medford*
Mayhew deacon William	do	Read Benjamin	do
Jernigan William jun.	do	Tufts James	do
Allen John Jun.	do	Rhodes Amos	*Lynn*
Peafe Martin	do	Robinfon James	do

[*The above Lift of Subfcribers, contains all the Names that were received previous to the commitment of this fheet to the prefs.*]

For EU product safety concerns, contact us at Calle de José Abascal, 56–1°,
28003 Madrid, Spain or eugpsr@cambridge.org.